Tackling Numeracy Issues

Book 2

Fractions, Decimals and Percentages

Key Stage 2

Caroline Clissold

The *Questions* Publishing Company Limited
Birmingham
2002

The Questions Publishing Company Ltd
Leonard House, 321 Bradford Street, Digbeth, Birmingham B5 6ET

First published in 2002

ISBN: 1-84190-047-8

Design by Al Stewart
Cover by Martin Cater and incidental illustrations by John Minett

Printed in the UK

Also available from The Questions Publishing Company Limited:

Book 1 *Fractions and Decimals, Key Stage 1*
ISBN: 1-84190-079-6

Book 3 *Fractions, Decimals, Percentages, Ratio and Proportion, Key Stage 2, Years 5 and 6*
ISBN: 1-84190-048-6

Book 4 Solving Maths Word Problems
ISBN: 1-84190-052-4

Book 5 *Improving the Plenary Session, Key Stage 1, Years 1 and 2*
ISBN: 1-84190-053-2

Book 6 *Improving the Plenary Session, Key Stage 2, Years 3 and 4*
ISBN: 1-84190-077-X

Book 7 *Improving the Plenary Session, Key Stage 2, Years 5 and 6*
ISBN: 1-84190-078-8

Contents

Definitions

Fraction
A part of something split into equal parts, made up of a numerator and denominator, for example $\frac{1}{4}$.

Decimal
A number like 0.2 and 3.25. They are 'part numbers', because they include amounts that are less than one.

Percentage
A special fraction that has a denominator of 100, like $\frac{67}{100}$. We write this as 67%. Per cent means 'for every hundred'.

Ratio
The relationship between two quantities, for example if we used 100 ml of juice and 300 ml of water to make a drink, the ratio would be 1:3 – one part of juice for every three parts of water.

Proportion
The relationship between measures or quantities, for example if there were ten dogs, three were wearing collars, the proportion wearing collars would be three in every ten. This can be expressed as a fraction or percentage, i.e. $\frac{3}{10}$ or 30%.

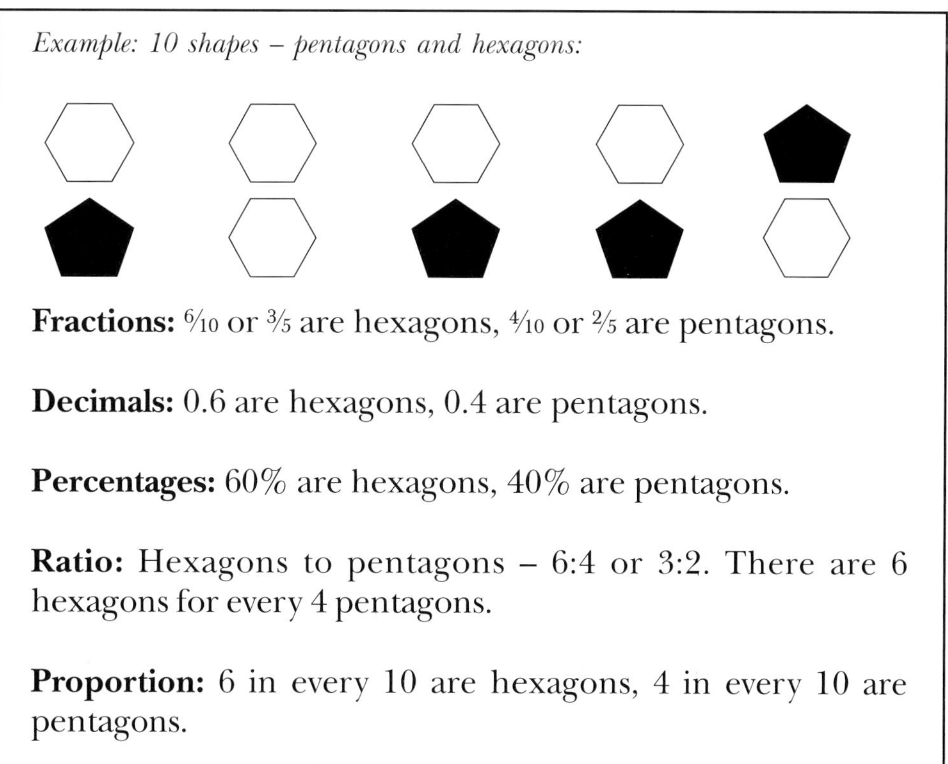

Example: 10 shapes – pentagons and hexagons:

Fractions: $\frac{6}{10}$ or $\frac{3}{5}$ are hexagons, $\frac{4}{10}$ or $\frac{2}{5}$ are pentagons.

Decimals: 0.6 are hexagons, 0.4 are pentagons.

Percentages: 60% are hexagons, 40% are pentagons.

Ratio: Hexagons to pentagons – 6:4 or 3:2. There are 6 hexagons for every 4 pentagons.

Proportion: 6 in every 10 are hexagons, 4 in every 10 are pentagons.

Introduction

The concepts of fractions, decimals, percentages, ratio and proportion are hard for children to understand. It is vital therefore that the foundations are laid for them early in their education and that these are secure within them, so that they can be built upon later.

In the **Foundation Stages**, which include Reception, children will develop an early experience of numbers through activities in real life or role-play contexts. They are introduced to the idea of half – half full, half past 10, share out the cubes so that you have half each, fold the paper in half, and so on. Initially, they will understand this as a part of something, rather than one of two equal parts. This will need reinforcement regularly, in order to help them to remember and begin to build that initial foundation block of fraction understanding.

Key Stage 1 progresses on from this, focusing on simple fractions (halves and quarters), decimals in the context of money, and early ideas of ratio and proportion.

In **Key Stage 2**, the ideas should be developed in a wide range of contexts, including practical work on money, measurement and problem solving.

Progression

The progression for this topic begins in the Early Years, but becomes a formal progression in Year 2. This is a very important year for the introduction of fractions as it provides the basis for future scaffolding. It is imperative that the children are given time for practical exploration of halves and quarters and are not rushed on too quickly to more complex fraction work.

It is important that children fully understand these concepts:

- halves and quarters of shapes and small numbers of objects;
- the equivalences between them, i.e. two halves and four quarters are both the same as a whole, one half and two quarters are the same.

Once this foundation has truly been built, the rest should come more easily. The children should not be moved on until a firm understanding of this initial concept has been achieved. At each stage in the children's progression through this topic it is important only to move on to the next step when they are ready.

Making links

Children and many adults often do not appreciate that fractions, decimals and percentages are equivalent ways of writing the same quantity and that fractions, decimals, percentages, ratio and proportion (FDPRP) are different ways of expressing related ideas.

To be an effective teacher of this topic, it is important to have a knowledge and awareness of the conceptual connections between these five ideas.

To develop into competent mathematicians, children need to understand the place of fractions and decimals in our number system: they need to be able to use the language of fractions confidently.

Many children have difficulty recognising equivalences in fractions, which is why it is very important to make these links at the earliest opportunity and regularly after that, beginning in Year 2 with quarters, halves and wholes.

Children also have difficulty making the links between fractions, decimals and percentages. Take every opportunity to help children appreciate these connections. Provide a range of practical contexts for children to explore and use FDPRP. Ensure that children see FDPRP expressed in different ways and appreciate that the representations are of related ideas.

To develop the children's understanding and the connections between these ideas, they need good experience of them in varied practical contexts and the links need to be explicit. Include, in your teaching, a wide range of opportunities to solve problems involving FDPRP in real-life contexts, money and measures.

When teaching FDPRP you need to be aware of the lines of progression in the numeracy framework and the aspects that children are likely to find difficult.

Common misconceptions

- Children are not always aware that fractions can be used in two ways: as a proportion of something, for example $\frac{1}{4}$ of £8; and as a fixed mark, for example $\frac{1}{2}$ is midway between 0 and 1.

- Many children do not recognise that fractions can be represented in several ways, for example $\frac{1}{4}$:

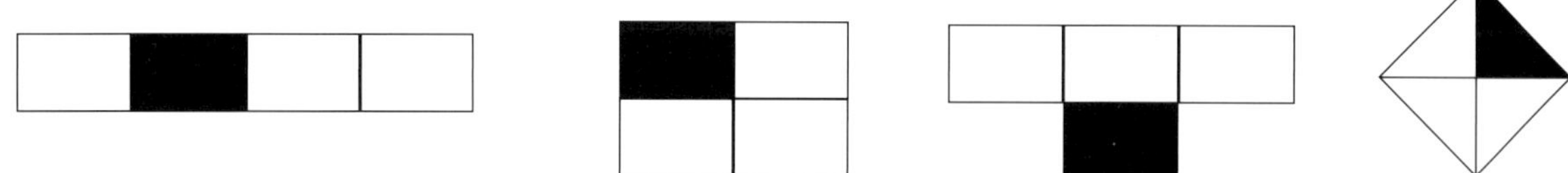

They need plenty of opportunities to experience this.

- Some children take a while to fully understand that when a whole is divided into fractions, each fraction is an equal part. For example, children may think that the following diagram shows fifths because there are five parts. They need to realise that because the parts are not equal, they are not fifths.

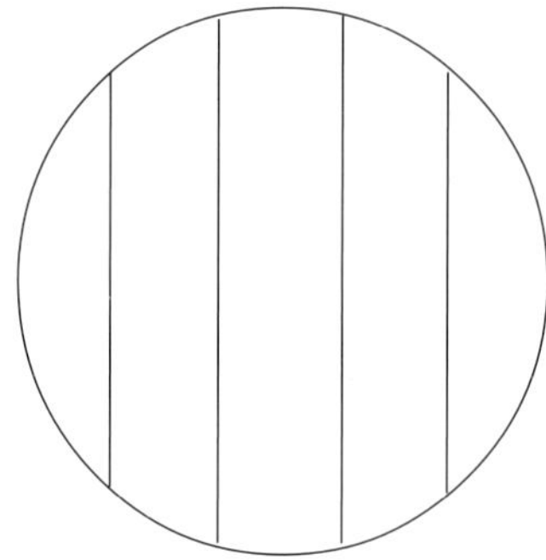

- Many children believe that the bigger the denominators that make up the fraction, the bigger the fraction is, for example $\frac{1}{5}$ is a larger fraction than $\frac{1}{3}$.

- Because multiplication makes numbers larger, many children think that this will happen to fractions – but in fact, multiplying a whole number by a fraction makes the answer smaller.

- Some children think that decimal numbers are larger than whole numbers because there are more digits, for example 2.145 is larger than 3.

Correct terms and notation

Numerator

The top number in a fraction, which shows us how many parts of something we have.

Denominator

The bottom number of a fraction, which shows us how many equal parts the whole has been divided into.

Proper fraction

A fraction where the numerator is less than the denominator.

Improper fraction

A fraction where the numerator is larger than the denominator.

Mixed number

A whole number with a proper fraction beside it, for example 3 ¼.

Vulgar fraction

The family word for all fractions.

Decimal fraction

The proper word for what we call a decimal.

Decimal point

This separates the whole numbers from the part numbers that are less than one.

Decimal place

The number of decimal places is the number of digits to the right of the decimal point, for example 12.75 has two decimal places.

Fractions

To develop an understanding of fractions, children must be given experiences that enable them to discover that fractions:

- are equal parts of a whole and that the number of parts gives the fraction its name;
- have equivalences and what these are;
- can be combined, compared, ordered and taken apart, and how this happens;
- are not ordinal numbers, i.e. an eighth is one part of a whole divided into eight, not the eighth position;
- of the same type are equal even if they appear to be different sizes, for example ½ of 24 = 12, ½ of 4 = 2, both are halves, it is the quantity that is different.

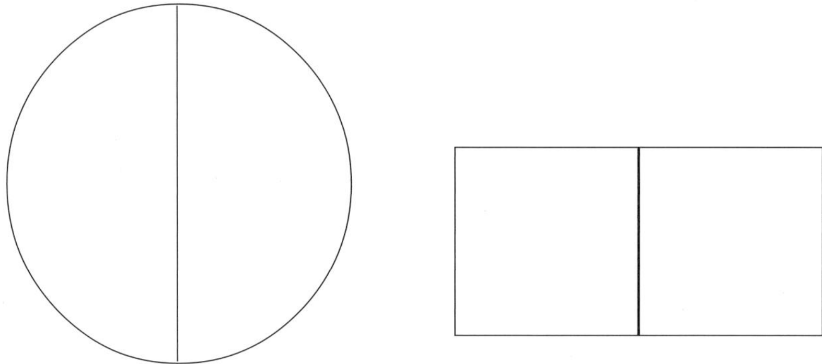

Children need to develop an understanding of the links between division and fractions, that if the numerator is divided by the denominator it will be converted into a decimal fraction and can sometimes be easier to understand or calculate as one. They need to develop their understanding of fraction vocabulary and be able to use this to discuss their work and record it.

This will all lead to a greater understanding of the addition, subtraction, multiplication and division of fractions, which will be important to them when they go to secondary school.

Decimal fractions

Initially, to help promote children's understanding, decimals are taught through money and measurement. Gradually children need to build up an understanding of decimals as parts of any whole numbers.

Work needs to be done on the place value of decimals, so that the children understand the concept of tenths being ten times smaller than a single digit unit and hundredths being one hundred times smaller. Practical activities involving the children are helpful, for example prepare some digit cards on A4 paper; include a decimal point. Give one child the decimal point, and give four others the digit cards. Ask them to make the largest number they can (by standing in the correct order), maybe 7532. Then ask them to divide it by 10, 100, multiply by 10, and so on. The children will need to place themselves around the decimal point. Make up new numbers from those digits and repeat the exercise.

When children are calculating mentally, they may use a strategy, for instance pretending the number is an amount of money, or pretending it is a whole number and then replacing the decimal point. This is acceptable as an efficient method of calculation, providing they understand the place value of the original number.

Addition, subtraction, multiplication and division of decimals come as a natural progression. If the children do not have a strong grasp of decimal fractions then they will not be experienced enough to tackle this next step. They will need to move back a stage in the progression and concentrate on becoming totally confident with decimals.

Percentages

Percentages are fractions whose denominator is 100, for example $\frac{12}{100}$. It is important that the children understand this concept and initially work with percentages as amounts out of 100. It is important to link common fractions with percentages, for example $\frac{1}{2} = 50\%$, $\frac{1}{4} = 25\%$. This should be done visually, with you as the teacher modelling this experience. Later on in this book there is an excellent example of how this can be done (see page 17). When the children have grasped this, move on to amounts out of 50 (by halving) and 200 (by doubling).

Next they need to be given experiences to develop an understanding of the relationship between fractions, decimals and percentages and the ability to convert from one to the other.

Common equivalences

These need teaching, so that the children learn them as facts:

$\frac{1}{2} = 0.5 = 50\%$

$\frac{1}{4} = 0.25 = 25\%$

$\frac{3}{4} = 0.75 = 75\%$

$\frac{1}{8} = 0.125 = 12\frac{1}{2}\%$

$\frac{1}{10} = 0.1 = 10\%$

Many other facts can be worked out from this knowledge.

Ratio and proportion

Ratio and proportion appear in the curriculum at Year 4. The children need very practical ways to experience them, for example investigating the proportions of colours used when mixing paints and practising ratio when exploring the scales on maps.

They need to understand that these are quantities that have a constant rule.

QCA demands

QCA's analysis of 1999 KS2 tests found that to raise standards, more effective teaching is needed in these areas:

- reducing fractions to their lowest form;
- ordering a set of mixed numbers;
- using decimal notation for tenths and hundredths;
- relating fractions to their decimal representations;
- finding simple percentages of small whole number quantities.

It also states that:

'Teachers should give a greater emphasis to place value when teaching decimals and not rely on money and measure context. Decimal place value has to be mastered in its own right.'

And:

'Children do not understand percentage as the number of parts per hundred, for example that 40% means 40 parts per hundred parts and that this can be written as the fraction $^{40}/_{100}$ or $^{4}/_{10}$ or $^{2}/_{5}$.'

One of the aims of this book is to help you, as the teacher, to teach these areas of fractions, decimals and percentages more effectively. It provides follow-up activities that will help to reinforce your teaching and enable the children to understand these concepts and to be able to make use of them in future 'real life' situations.

Excellent teaching

The following suggestions offer some thoughts to have in mind while you plan.

Excellent teaching occurs when:

- lessons are kept simple and there are effective, but not too many, resources;
- there is space for direct teaching;
- there is correct use of vocabulary and phrasing from both teacher and child;
- there is questioning, and answers are given, in sentences;
- modelling and demonstrating are done using the equipment the children are expected to use;
- step-by-step teaching is employed;
- objectives are shared between teacher and children;
- there are high expectations;
- planning has been well thought out.

The activities in this book are designed to help you teach fractions, decimals, percentages, ratio and proportion effectively. Most of the ideas can be adapted to use in different year groups and with different abilities of children.

The following is the National Numeracy Strategy's progression through fractions, decimals, percentages, ratio and proportion. Year 2 to Year 6 has been included to provide an overview of the whole progression throughout this topic. Although you may be responsible for one particular year group it is important to have a sense of the requirements of children at each step of Key Stage 2. This will help you to understand how children develop their knowledge of these concepts. The most important point to remember is that as a teacher you must ensure that the children in your class have a complete and full understanding of an objective before you move them on.

Progression through fractions, decimals, percentages, ratios and proportion

Year 2

- Begin to recognise and find one half and one quarter of shapes and numbers of objects.
- Begin to recognise that two halves or four quarters make one whole and that two quarters and one half are equivalent.

Year 3

- Recognise unit fractions such as ½, ⅓, ¼, ⅕, ⅒, and use them to find fractions of shapes and numbers.
- Begin to recognise simple fractions that are several parts of a whole, such as ¾, ⅔ or 3⁄10.
- Begin to recognise simple equivalent fractions: for example, five tenths and one half, five fifths and one whole.
- Compare familiar fractions: for example, know that on the number line one half lies between one quarter and three quarters.
- Estimate a simple fraction.

Year 4

- Use fraction notation.
- Recognise simple fractions that are several parts of a whole, such as ⅔ or ⅝, and mixed numbers, such as 5¾.
- Recognise the equivalence of simple fractions (for example, fractions equivalent to ½, ¼ or ¾).
- Identify two simple fractions with a total of 1, for example 3⁄10 and 7⁄10.
- Order simple fractions: for example, decide whether fractions such as ⅜ or 7⁄10 are greater or less than one half.
- Begin to relate fractions to division and find simple fractions such as ½, ⅓, ¼, ⅕, ⅒ of numbers or quantities. Find fractions such as ⅔, ¾, ⅗, 7⁄10 of shapes.
- Begin to use ideas of simple proportion: for example, one for every . . . and one in every . . .

- Understand decimal notation and place value for tenths and hundredths, and use it in context: for example, order amounts of money; convert a sum of money such as £13.25 to pence, or a length such as 125cm to metres; round a sum of money to the nearest pound.
- Recognise the equivalence between the decimal and the fraction forms of one half and one quarter, and tenths such as 0.3.

Year 5

- Use fraction notation, including mixed numbers and the vocabulary numerator and denominator.
- Change an improper fraction into a mixed number, for example change $^{13}/_{10}$ to $1^{3}/_{10}$.
- Recognise when two simple fractions are equivalent, including relating hundredths to tenths, for example $^{70}/_{100} = {}^{7}/_{10}$.
- Order a set of fractions such as 2, $2^{3}/_{4}$, $1^{3}/_{4}$, $2^{1}/_{2}$, and position them on a number line.
- Relate fractions to division, and use division to find simple fractions, including tenths and hundredths, of numbers and quantities, for example $^{3}/_{4}$ of 12, $^{1}/_{10}$ of 50, $^{1}/_{100}$ of £3.
- Solve simple problems using ideas of ratio and proportion (one for every . . . one in every . . .).
- Use decimal notation for tenths and hundredths.
- Know what each digit represents in a number with two decimal places.
- Order a set of numbers or measurements with the same number of decimal places.
- Round a number with one or two decimal places to the nearest integer.
- Relate fractions to their decimal representations, for example $^{1}/_{2} = 0.5$, $^{1}/_{4} = 0.25$, $^{3}/_{4} = 0.75$, and tenths and hundredths such as $^{7}/_{10} = 0.7$, $^{27}/_{100} = 0.27$.
- Begin to understand percentage as the number of parts in every 100, and find simple percentages of whole-number quantities, for example 25% of £8.
- Express one half, one quarter, three quarters and tenths and hundredths, as percentages, for example $^{3}/_{4} = 75\%$.

Year 6

- Change a fraction such as $^{33}/_{8}$ to the equivalent mixed number $4^{1}/_{8}$ and vice versa.
- Recognise relationships between fractions, for example $^{1}/_{10}$ is ten times $^{1}/_{100}$, and $^{1}/_{16}$ is half of $^{1}/_{8}$.
- Reduce a fraction to its simplest form by cancelling common factors in the numerator and denominator.
- Order fractions such as $^{2}/_{3}$, $^{3}/_{4}$, and $^{5}/_{6}$ by converting them to fractions with a common denominator and position them on a number line.
- Use a fraction (including tenths and hundredths) as an operator to find fractions of numbers or quantities, for example $^{5}/_{8}$ of 32, $^{7}/_{10}$ of 40, $^{9}/_{100}$ of 400cm.
- Solve simple problems involving ratio and proportion.
- Use decimal notation for tenths and hundredths in calculations, and tenths, hundredths and thousandths when recording measurements.
- Know what each digit represents in a number with up to three decimal places.
- Give a decimal fraction lying between two others, for example between 3.4 and 3.5.
- Order a mixed set of numbers or measurements with up to three decimal places.
- Round a number with two decimal places to the nearest tenth or whole number.
- Recognise the equivalence between the decimal and fraction forms of one half, one quarter, one eighth and tenths, hundredths and thousandths, for example $^{700}/_{1000} = {}^{70}/_{100} = {}^{7}/_{10} = 0.7$.
- Begin to convert a fraction to a decimal using division.
- Understand percentages as the number of parts in every 100. Express simple fractions such as one half, one quarter, three quarters, one third, two thirds and tenths and hundredths as percentages, for example know that $^{1}/_{3} = 33\ ^{1}/_{3}\%$.
- Find simple percentages of small whole-number quantities, for example find 10% of £500, then 20%, 40% and 80% by doubling.

Ready reference table: Book 2

Chapter	Numeracy Strategy	National Curriculum
1 Fraction strips	Year 3 to Year 6	Key Stage 2/2d Key Stage 2/2e
2 Dominoes	Year 3 to Year 6	Key Stage 2/2d Key Stage 2/2e
3 'Show me' strips	Year 3 to Year 6 Year 4 to Year 6	Key Stage 2/2d Key Stage 2/2e Key Stage 2/2f Key Stage 2/2i
4 Bingo	Year 3 to Year 6 Year 4 to Year 6	Key Stage 2/2d Key Stage 2/2e Key Stage 2/2f Key Stage 2/2i
5 Clock fractions	Year 3 to Year 6	Key Stage 2/2d Key Stage 2/2e
6 Brainstorming fractions and percentages	Year 3 to Year 6 Years 5 and 6	Key Stage 2/2d Key Stage 2/2f
7 Make a whole	Year 3 to Year 6	Key Stage 2/2d Key Stage 2/2e
8 Halving patterns	Year 3 to Year 6	Key Stage 2/2d Key Stage 2/2e
9 Fraction sticks	Year 3 to Year 6	Key Stage 2/2d Key Stage 2/2e
10 Go for five	Year 3 to Year 6 Years 5 and 6	Key Stage 2/2d Key Stage 2/2e Key Stage 2/2f Key Stage 2/2i

Chapter 1

Fraction strips

These are a very practical, visual and manageable way of helping the children to compare fractions and order them.

Select the fractions that you want to focus on:

- Year 2: whole, halves and quarters;
- Year 3: whole, halves, thirds, quarters, fifths and tenths;
- Year 4: whole, halves, thirds, quarters, fifths, eighths, tenths;
- Year 5 and 6: all of those provided.

Preparation
Photocopy photocopiable sheet 1 and cut out the strips appropriate for your year.

Children working on this activity will need their own set of strips.

You will need a set photocopied onto A3 paper or acetates if using an OHP for demonstration purposes.

Colour one part of each fraction so that comparisons will be clearer, for example:

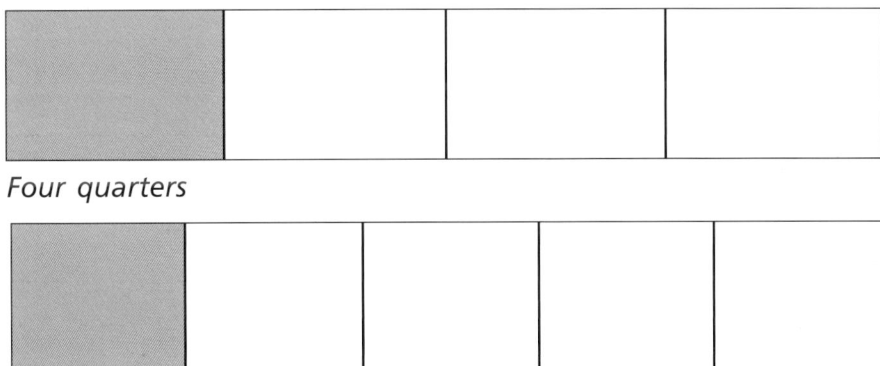

Four quarters

Five fifths

Photocopy the fraction cards and number lines, photocopiable sheets 2 and 3.

Introduction
Discuss with the children what fractions the strips you are focusing on have been split into. Ask such questions as:

How can you tell what the fraction is? What is special about each section of the strip?

Now look at the two strips and ask the following questions:

Which is the largest fraction?
Why is it larger when the numbers are smaller?
How many of the fraction are needed to make the whole strip?
How many are needed to make half the strip?
Are $\frac{2}{4}$ larger/smaller/equal to $\frac{2}{5}$?

Lots of questioning about the fractions is needed.

Compare three or four similar strips, selecting according to your year group, for example, for Year 4 use whole, halves, quarters and eighths. Use your A3 copies, stick them onto the board or use the acetates and OHP:

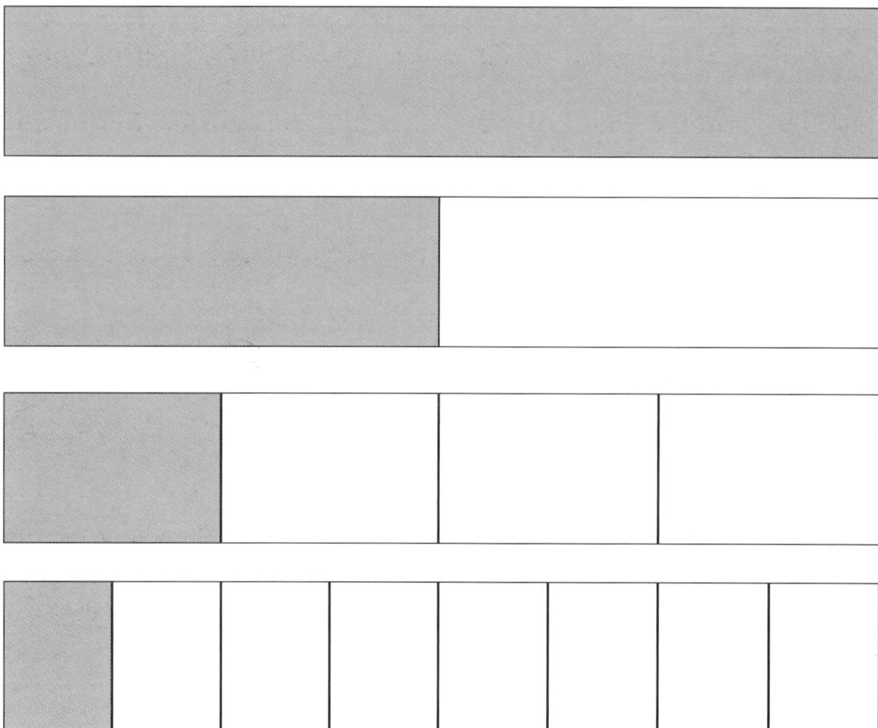

Key questions

- How many quarters are the same as a m?
- How many eighths are the same as q?
- Which is greater, m or q?
- What fraction of p is x?'

Activities

Working in groups, give the children sets of fraction cards and ask them to use their fraction strips to compare the sizes and order them from smallest to largest on a number line.

Example: use these fraction cards

This group will need the fractions strips for halves, thirds, quarters and fifths.

Once they have ordered the cards, they should then transfer this information onto a number line:

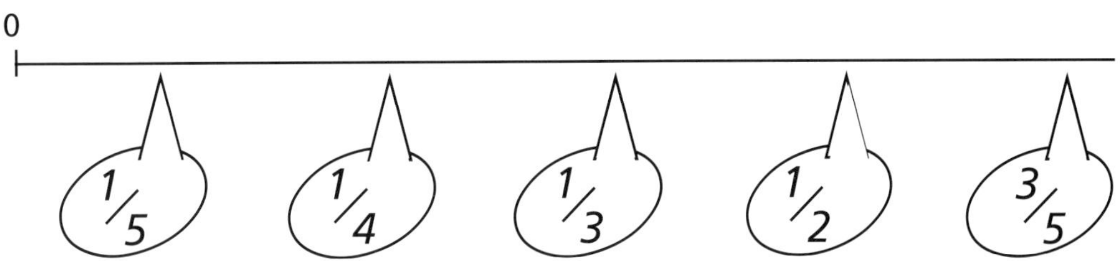

At this stage, it is helpful not to put 1 at the other end of the line, as the children need to focus on ordering the fractions and not positioning them in the correct place on a 0 to 1 line. Alternatively use a number line like this:

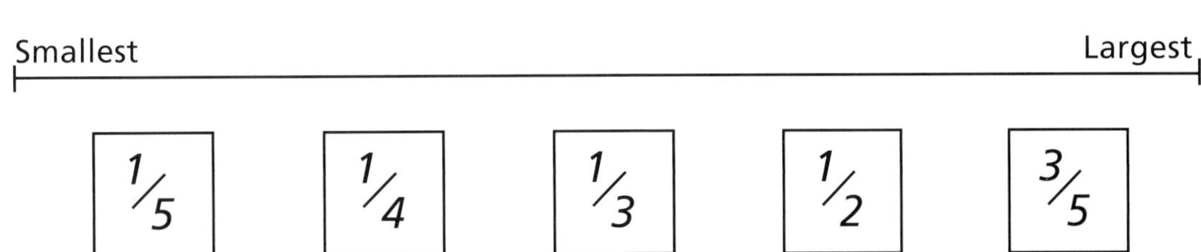

This type of activity needs plenty of repetition with a variety of fraction cards.

Photocopiable Sheet 1

Set of fraction strips

One whole

Two halves

Three thirds

Four quarters

Five fifths

Six sixths

Seven sevenths

Eight eighths

Nine ninths

Ten tenths

Photocopiable Sheet 2
Fraction cards

Use from 3 to 6 at a time, maybe more for older and/or more able children.

Year 2

Year 3

3/4

3/10

Year 4: all the above plus

Years 5 and 6: all the Year 3 and 4 selections plus

6/7
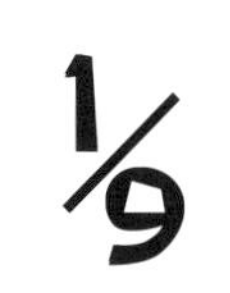

3/9

Photocopiable Sheet 3

Number lines

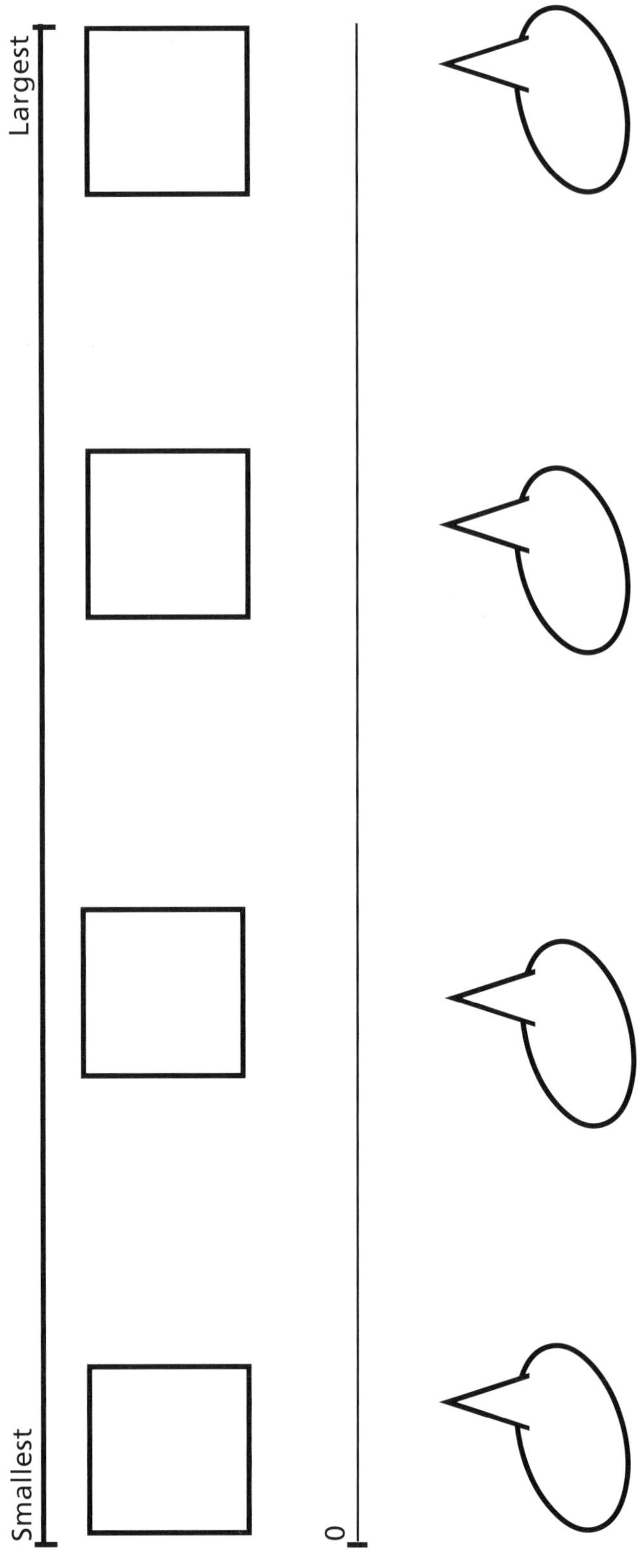

Largest

Smallest

0

Chapter 2

Dominoes

Dominoes can be a very flexible resource. Photocopy sheets 5 and 6 onto card and cut out. They can be used by individual children in pairs or groups. They are also a valuable demonstration tool when used on acetate with an OHP.

Preparation

Photocopy the dominoes onto acetate and cut them out for use with an OHP. Photocopy sets onto card for the children to use in order to model what you are demonstrating, i.e. if you are demonstrating equivalent fractions, ask the children for suggestions for you to show on acetate, and then ask the children to find them, or others that follow the same criteria.

Activities

> The following photocopiable sheets can be used for any of the activities below, differentiated as required. Select the dominoes required from those printed on photocopiable sheets 5 and 6 for use in teaching particular objectives. For guidance as to the appropriate fractions for each age group, see Chapter 1.

1. Sorting

Sort dominoes according to these criteria:

- even numerators;
- odd numerators;
- even denominators;
- odd denominators;
- those equalling a whole, for example:

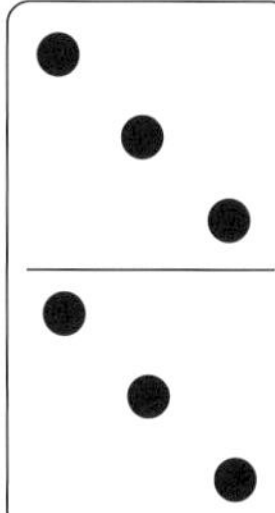

- those equalling 1/2, for example:

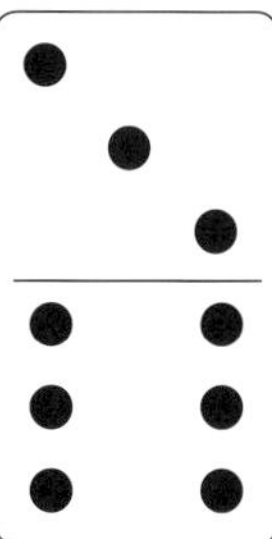

- those less than a half;
- those that can be mixed numbers, for example:

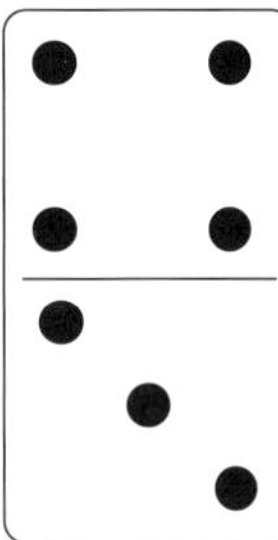

This is a good exercise for demonstrating mixed number fractions – how many wholes and how many left over?

- equivalent fractions, for example:

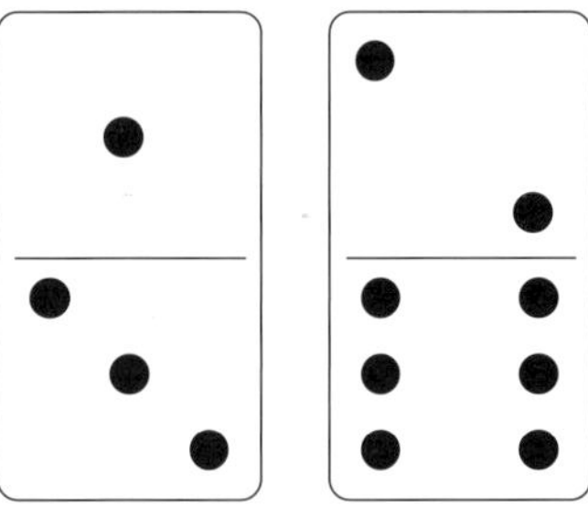

Key questions

- What is the numerator?
- What is the denominator?
- What is an equivalent fraction?
- What do we mean by a mixed number fraction?
- Can you give us an example?
- What would happen if we turned the domino the other way around?
- How do you know this?
- Can you come and show us another example on the OHP?

2. Making links

Play the game of dominoes with one of these rules:

a) connect one domino to another so that a mixed fraction is made;

b) the numerator is even;

c) the fraction made can be identified as an equivalent fraction to another made up by the player, etc.

3. Ordering

Choose a selection of dominoes, place them vertically and order them from smallest to largest. Copy onto a number line, e.g.

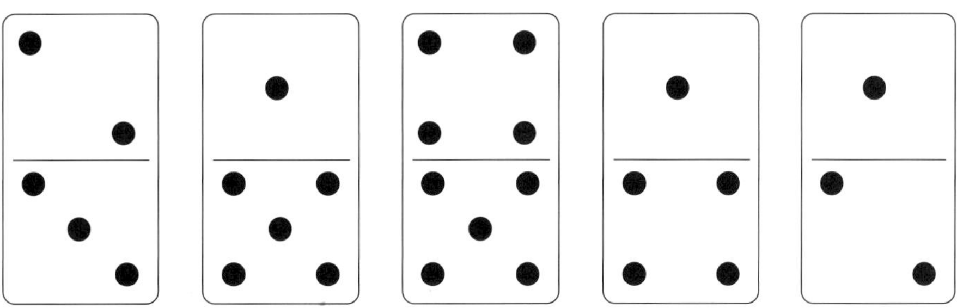

Photocopiable Sheet 4

Lining up dominoes

Largest

Smallest

Photocopiable Sheet 5
Dominoes A

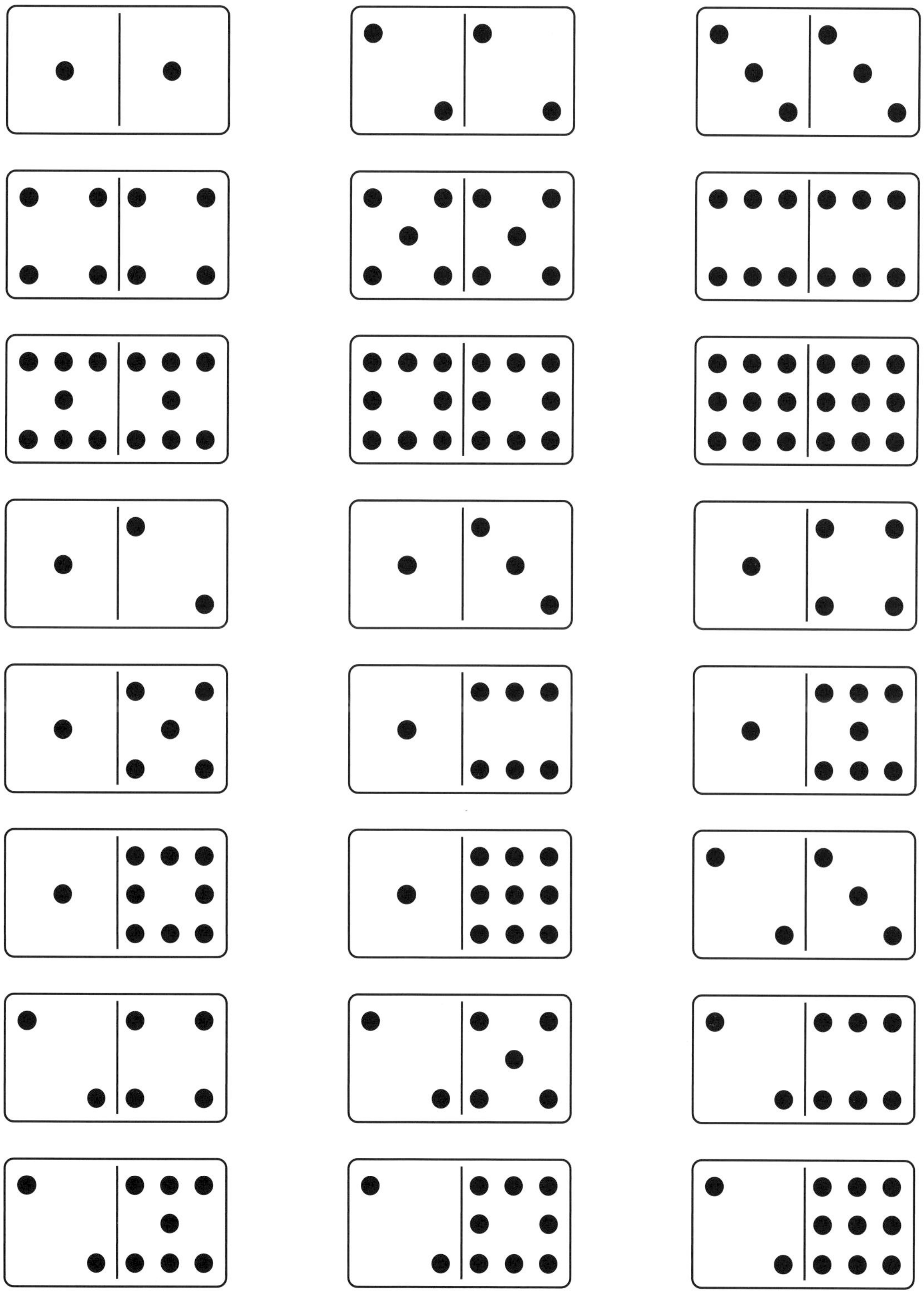

Photocopiable Sheet 6

Dominoes B

Photocopiable Sheet 7

Dominoes 1

Draw dominoes that have even numerators and odd denominators.

Example:

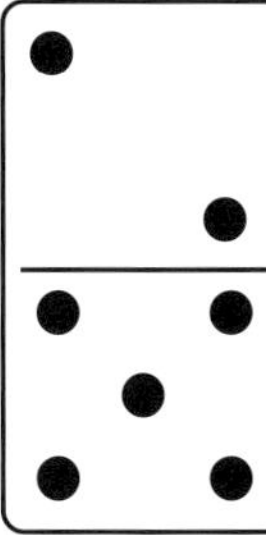

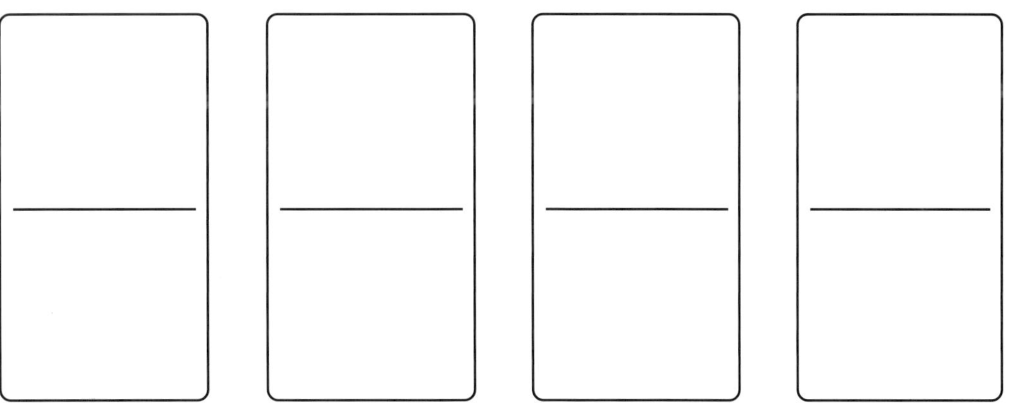

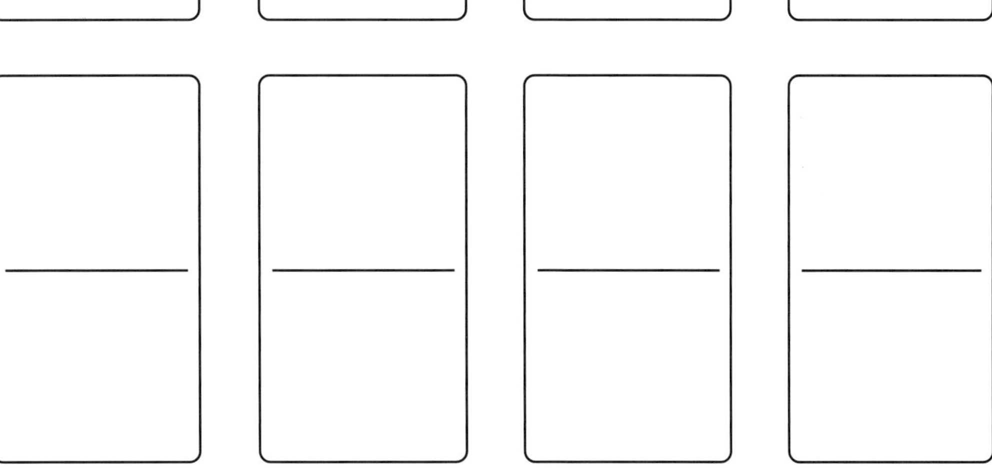

Photocopiable Sheet 8
Dominoes 2

Draw dominoes that equal a whole.

Example:

Photocopiable Sheet 9
Dominoes 3

Draw dominoes that are mixed numbers and write down the whole number and left-over fraction.

Example:

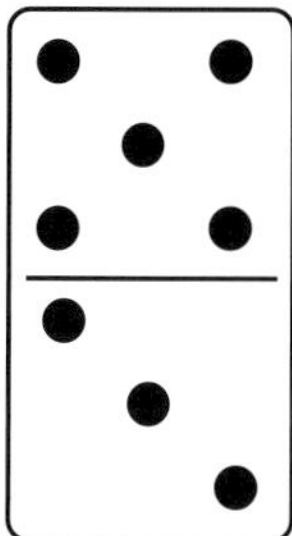

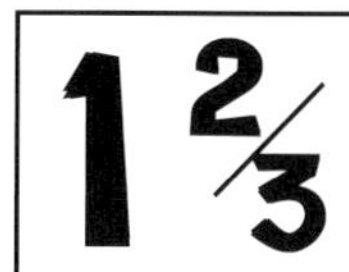

1.

2.

3.

4.

5.

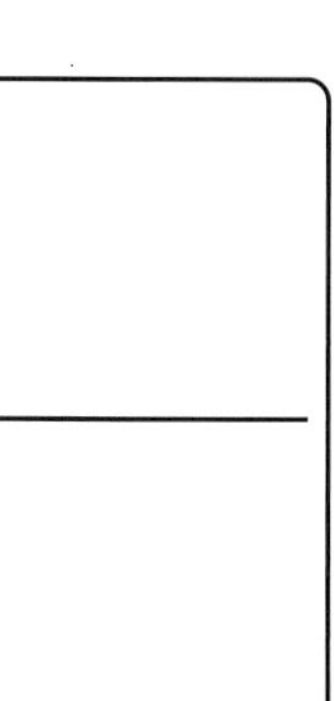

6.

Photocopiable Sheet 10

Dominoes 4

Draw dominoes that are equivalent to each other and label them.

Example:

$\frac{1}{2}$ and $\frac{2}{4}$

Now draw and label some of your own on the back of this sheet.

Chapter 3

'Show me' strips

These are a wonderful resource for all sorts of activities. Here we will be thinking of the links between fractions, decimals and percentages.

The 'show me' strip is a strip of card divided into ten parts. The children use a paper clip to slide up and down the strip to wherever you ask them to go, for example, imagine one end of the strip is 0 and the other is 1, you might ask the children to show you where $\frac{1}{2}$ would be. They would put the paper clip in the middle on the fifth line. For 75%, it would go half way between the 7th and 8th lines, for $\frac{2}{5}$, it would go on the 4th line, and so on.

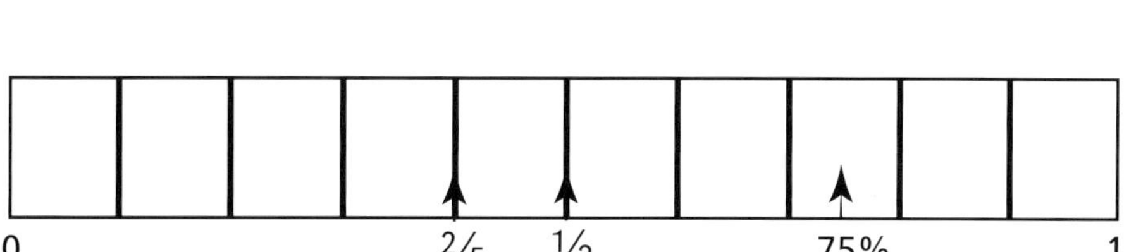

Preparation

Photocopy enough 'show me' strips from photocopiable sheet 11 for each child to be able to use one. Attach a paper clip to each or a tight elastic band if you prefer. Copy the appropriate activity sheet for each child – photocopiable sheet 12 for Year 3, photocopiable sheet 13 for Year 4 and photocopiable sheet 14 for Years 5/6.

Oral and mental starter activity

During oral and mental starters with Year 4, 5 and 6 children, ask them to find and show you a mixture of fractions, decimals and percentages on these strips. Ask them to show you equivalences, for example $\frac{1}{10}$, $\frac{2}{5}$, 40%, 0.4, so that they have reinforcement and rehearsal of this concept.

Whole-class/group-work session activities

A simple but effective lesson could involve the children showing fractions, decimals and percentages on their 'show me' strips and then drawing their work on 'show me' grids as follows:

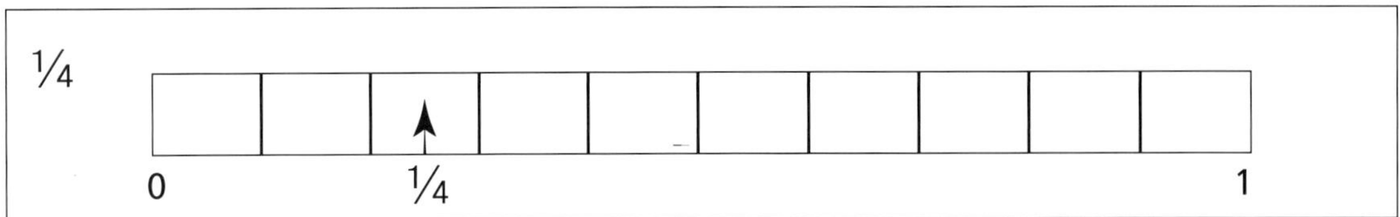

Make the fractions, decimals and percentages appropriate to the age or ability of the children.

- **Year 2:** whole, halves and quarters;
- **Year 3:** whole, halves, thirds, quarters, fifths and tenths;
- **Year 4:** whole, halves, thirds, quarters, fifths, eighths, tenths and decimals to tenths;
- **Year 5 and 6:** all the above, and decimals to hundredths and percentages.

The following activity sheets are designed to either be used as shown or to be adapted to suit the children in your class.

Key questions

- What would this be as a decimal?
- What would this be as a fraction?
- Can you think of an equivalent fraction?
- What would this be as a percentage?
- Is this amount smaller or larger than the last one?
- How do you know?
- Can you think of as many amounts as possible that would go here?

Photocopiable Sheet 11
'Show me' strips A

Copy these three strips onto card and then cut them out.

Photocopiable Sheet 12

'Show me' strips B

Year 3

Show these fractions on your 'show me' strip and then plot them on the 'show me' strips below. The first one has been done for you.

$3/4$

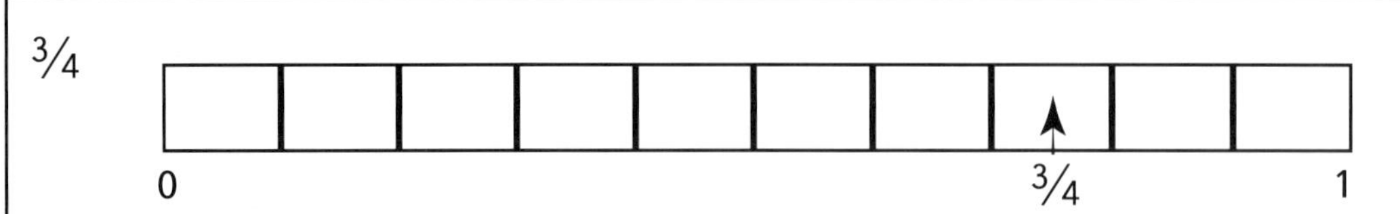

$1/2$

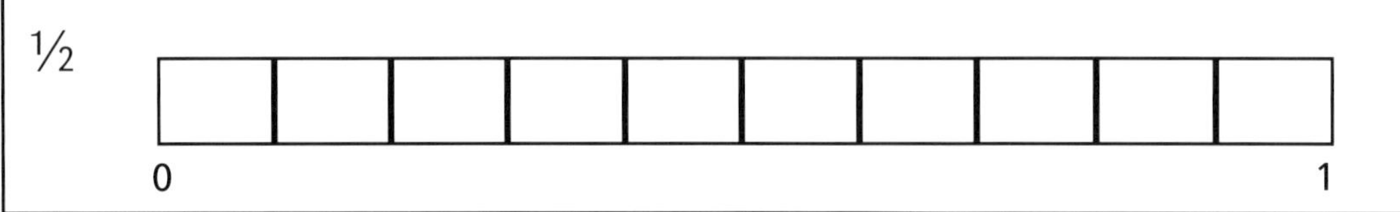

$7/10$

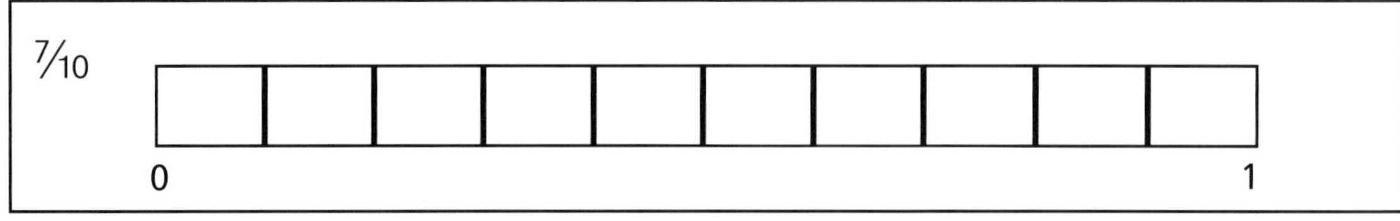

$3/5$

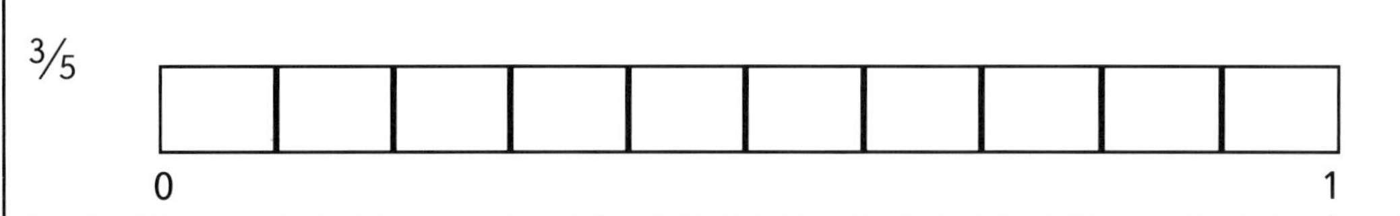

$4/5$

0 1

$3/10$

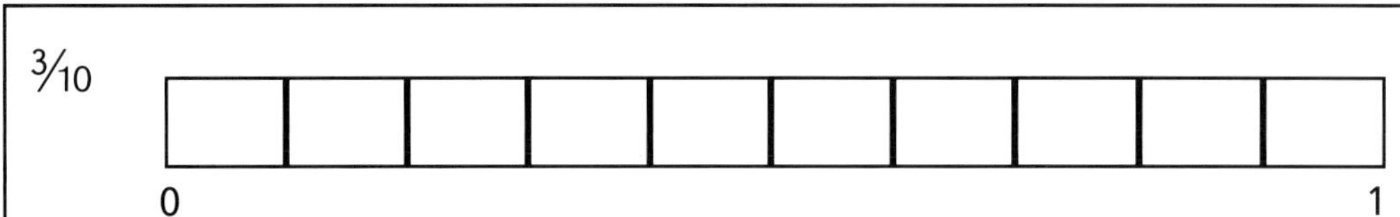

$1/4$

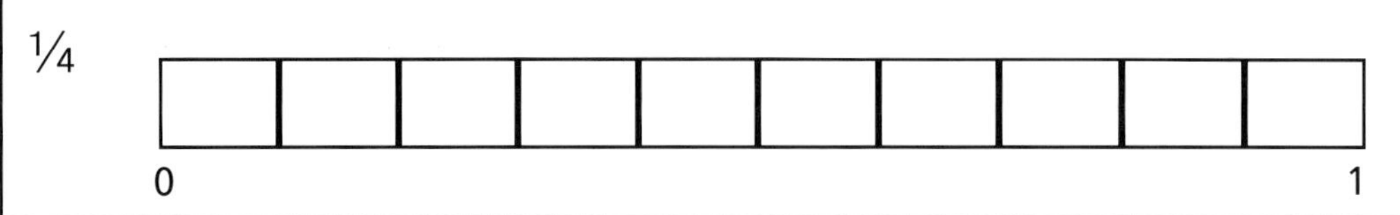

$5/10$

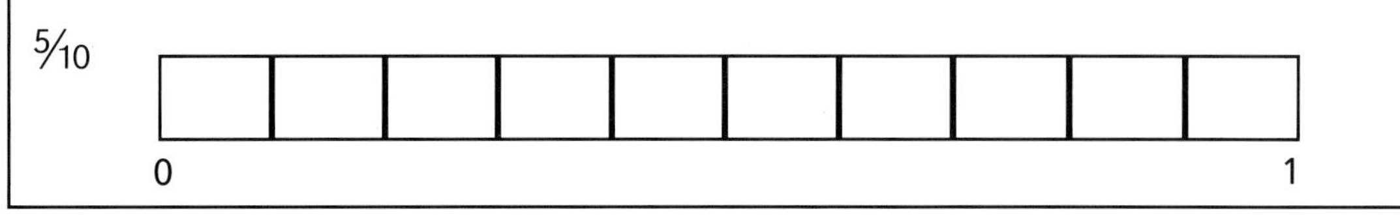

Photocopiable Sheet 13

'Show me' strips C

Year 4

Show these fractions and decimals on your 'show me' strip and then plot them on the 'show me' strips below. The first one has been done for you.

0.4

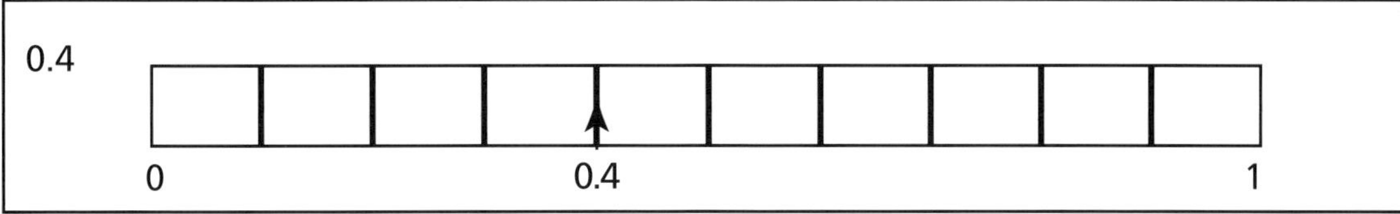

$\frac{1}{5}$

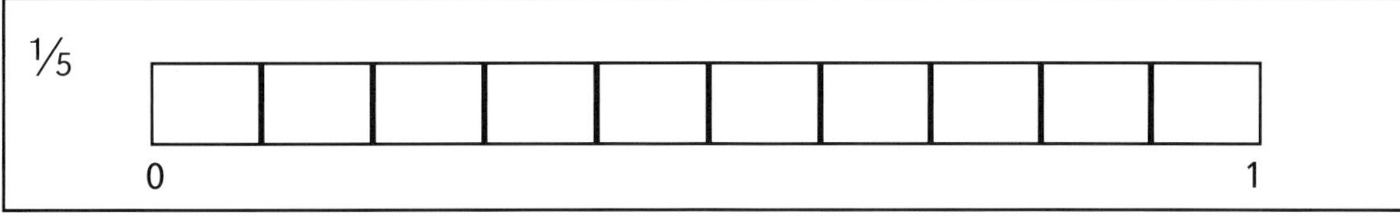

0.75

0 1

$\frac{3}{4}$

0 1

$\frac{4}{5}$

0 1

$\frac{3}{10}$

0 1

0.6

0 1

$\frac{5}{10}$

0 1

Photocopiable Sheet 14
'Show me' strips D

Year 5/6

Show these fractions, decimals and percentages on your 'show me' strips and then plot them on the 'show me' strips below.

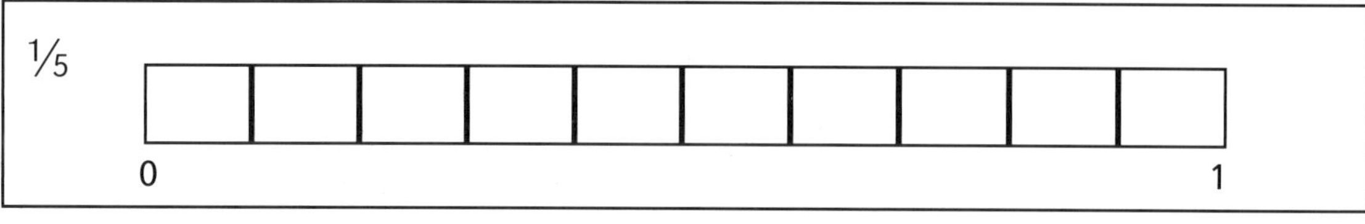

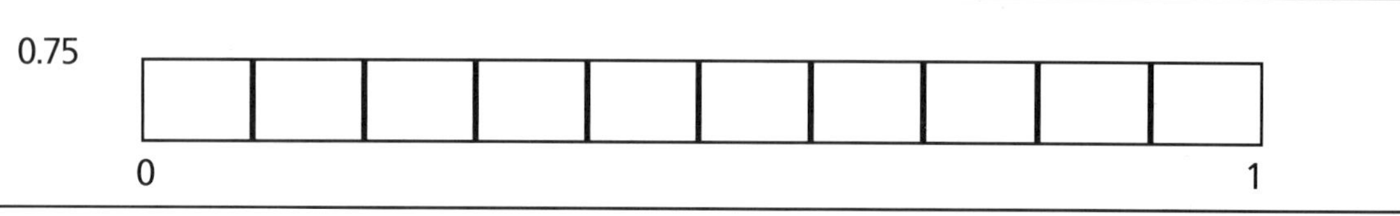

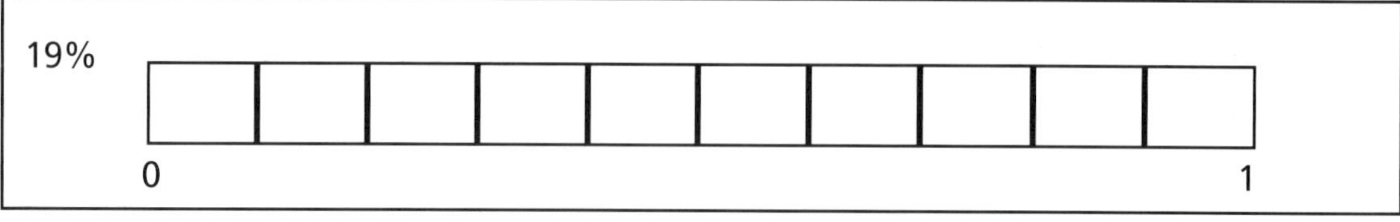

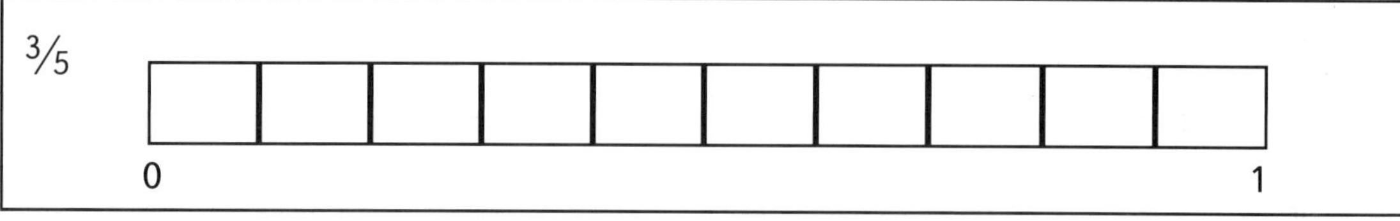

3/20

0 1

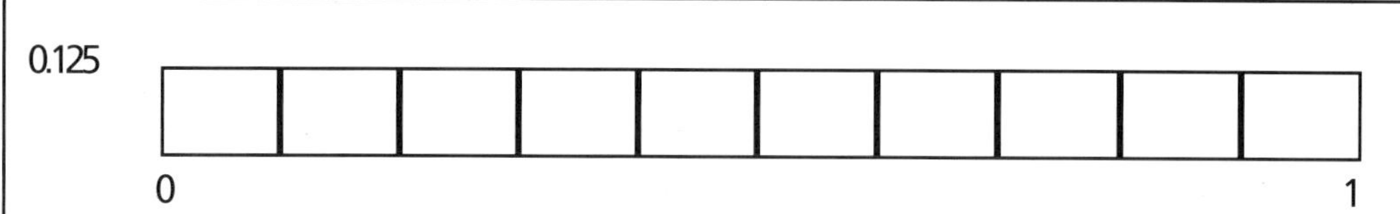

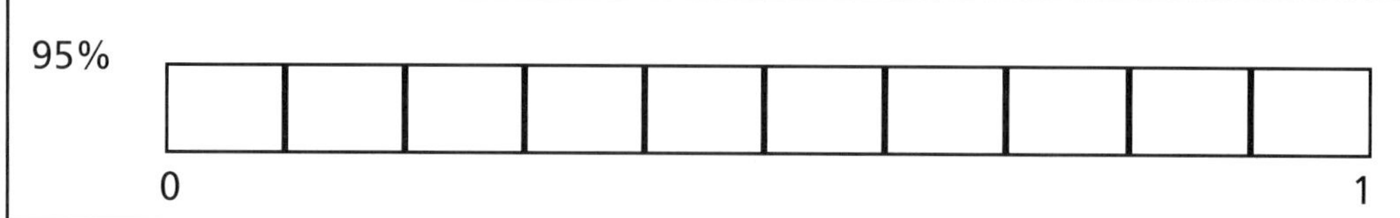

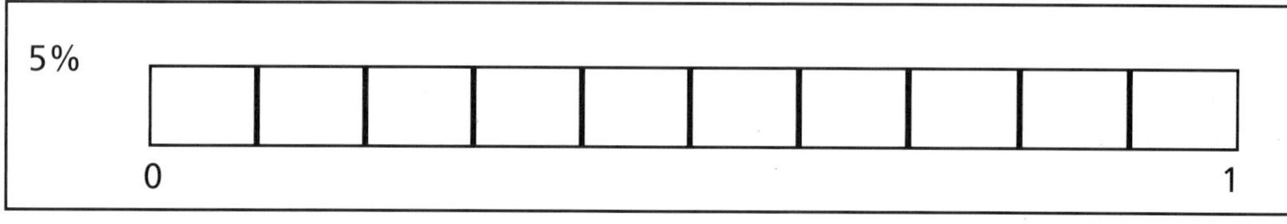

Chapter 4

Bingo

This is a quick game to help reinforce the links between fractions, decimals and percentages. It could be played as part of the oral and mental starter or plenary sessions.

Preparation

The children will need a four by three blank grid. Photocopy those on photocopiable sheet 15.

Sample questions for each year group are provided on the following pages.

Activity

Give a copy of a grid from photocopiable sheet 15 to each child.

The children should fill in the grid with either numbers or fractions, decimals and percentages as specified by you, for example numbers between 10 and 50. You then call out questions and if they have a number that answers your question, they cross it out, for example, 'What is $\frac{1}{4}$ of 40?' If they have 10 on their grid, they cross it out. The winner is the first player to cross out all their numbers correctly. If they do not have the answer to your question on their grid, they do not cross anything out.

Some numbers may be able to be crossed out twice. This is of no benefit other than encouraging the children to consider all the numbers each time.

Questions should be a mixture of those requiring one specific answer and more general ones that enable the children to cross out several numbers at a time. Questions should include a range of difficulty, from simple to challenging for the most able children. The children could play in mixed ability pairs, which will help the lower achieving children.

Example: Year 2

Ask the children to fill their grid with 12 numbers between 10 and 50.

The questions are linked to halves and quarters.

~~25~~	30	50	36
~~40~~	16	21	48
~~15~~	18	12	28

Questions

1. ¼ of 40. (Not on my grid)
2. ¾ of 40 (30)
3. ½ of 26 (13, not on my grid)
4. Cross out any numbers that can be divided into quarters.
   (36, 40, 16, 48, 12, 28)
5. ½ of 100. (50)
6. ½ of 50. (25)
7. Cross out any numbers that cannot be halved. (21, 15)
8. ½ of 22. (Not on my grid)
9. ½ of me is 9, what number am I? (18)
10. ½ of me is 7, what number am I? (14, not on my grid)
11. ¼ of me is 8, what number am I? (32, not on my grid)
12. ¾ of me is 16, what number am I? (20, not on my grid)
13. ½ of 88. (44, not on my grid)
14. ¼ of 88. (22, not on my grid)
15. ¼ of 104. (26, not on my grid)
16. ½ of 60. (30)

BINGO!

Example: Year 3

Ask the children to fill their grids with numbers between 10 and 100. Questions should be linked to halves, thirds, quarters, fifths and tenths.

Questions

1. $\frac{1}{5}$ of 50.
2. $\frac{1}{2}$ of 200.
3. $\frac{1}{4}$ of 100.
4. $\frac{1}{2}$ of 82.
5. $\frac{1}{2}$ of 34.
6. $\frac{1}{3}$ of 120.
7. $\frac{1}{4}$ of 44.
8. $\frac{1}{3}$ of 39.
9. $\frac{1}{2}$ of 32.
10. $\frac{1}{2}$ of me is 22, what number am I?
11. $\frac{1}{2}$ of me is 43, what number am I?
12. $\frac{1}{4}$ of me is 20, what number am I?
13. $\frac{3}{4}$ of me is 15, what number am I?
14. $\frac{1}{5}$ of me is 12, what number am I?
15. $\frac{2}{5}$ of me is 4, what number am I?
16. Cross out all the numbers that can be divided into fifths.
17. Cross out all the numbers that can be divided into thirds.
18. Cross out all the numbers that can be divided into halves.

BINGO!

Example: Year 4

Ask the children to fill their grids with multiples of 3 and 4 up to 50. Questions should be linked to Year 3 fractions plus eighths and decimals.

Questions

1. $\frac{1}{2}$ of 30.

2. $\frac{2}{3}$ of 30.

3. $\frac{1}{3}$ of 12.

4. $\frac{1}{3}$ of 9.

5. $\frac{1}{4}$ of 32.

6. $\frac{1}{4}$ of 64.

7. $\frac{3}{4}$ of 40.

8. $\frac{1}{5}$ of 200.

9. $\frac{2}{5}$ of 60.

10. $\frac{1}{8}$ of 48.

11. Cross out numbers that can be divided into fifths.

12. $\frac{3}{4}$ of me is 16, what is my number?

13. $\frac{4}{8}$ of me is 12, what is my number?

14. $\frac{1}{2}$ of 50 plus $\frac{1}{2}$ of 40.

15. 23.4 + 20.6.

16. 13.5 + 13.5.

17. Cross out numbers that can be divided into both halves and thirds.

18. Cross out numbers that can be divided into eighths.

BINGO!

Example: Year 5

Ask the children to fill their grids with multiples of 6 and 7 up to 100. Questions should be linked to Year 3 fractions, sixths, eighths, percentages and decimals.

Questions

1. $\frac{1}{7}$ of me is 7, what number am I?
2. 20% of 70.
3. $\frac{1}{6}$ of 72.
4. $\frac{5}{6}$ of 72.
5. $\frac{1}{8}$ of 56.
6. $\frac{3}{8}$ of 56.
7. $\frac{5}{8}$ of 56.
8. $\frac{1}{2}$ of 112.
9. $\frac{1}{4}$ of 280.
10. $\frac{1}{4}$ of me is 18, what number am I?
11. I am 4 times as big as 16.5, what am I?
12. $\frac{1}{5}$ of 45 plus $\frac{1}{3}$ of 27.
13. Cross out any numbers that can be divided into both quarters and sixths.
14. Cross out any numbers that can be divided into both thirds and sevenths.
15. Cross out any numbers that are 25% of any number up to 60.
16. Cross out any numbers that can be divided into both fifths and sixths.
17. Cross out any numbers that can be divided into both sixths and twelfths.
18. Cross out any numbers between 25.5 and 30.5.

BINGO!

Example: Year 6

Ask the children to fill their grids with mixed whole and part numbers between 1 and 10. Questions should be linked to previous year's fractions, percentages and decimals.

Questions

1. ⅓ of 1.5.

2. ¼ of 10.

3. Cross out any numbers that come between 3.7 and 4.2.

4 ½ of 7.

5. Cross out any numbers that have eighths or its equivalent.

6. Cross out any numbers that come between 1.7 and 2.5.

7. 10% of 50 plus 1% of 200.

8. 5% of 65.

9. 1% of 650.

10. 20% of 50.

11. Cross out any numbers that will become whole numbers if they are multiplied by 10.

12. Cross out any whole numbers that become part numbers when divided by 2.

13. I am 10 times as big as 0.8, what number am I?

14. I am 20 times as big as 0.45, what number am I?

15. ⅛ of 60.

16. Cross out any numbers that have .2 or its equivalent.

17. I am 3 times as big as 2.75, what number am I?

18. Cross out any numbers that have ¼ or its equivalent.

BINGO!

Photocopiable Sheet 15

Bingo grids

Chapter 5

Clock fractions

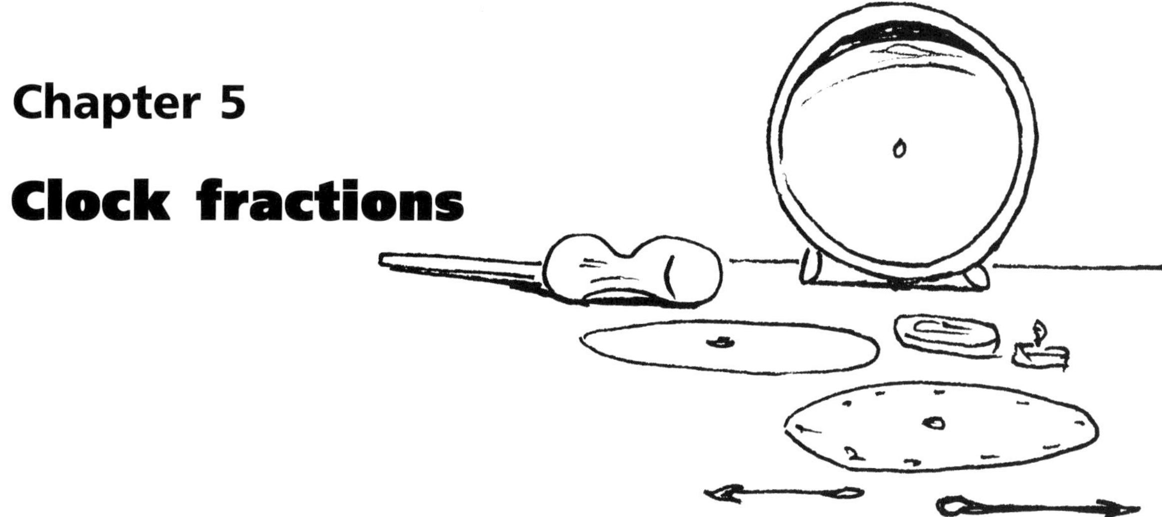

Clocks make a good demonstration tool for teaching equivalent fractions. For Year 2 children, the activities should be used after they have been introduced to time and practical clock-work.

Preparation

The children will need a small clock each.

You will need an acetate copy of the clock on photocopiable sheet 16 to use with an OHP and several copies on A4 card. Cut these into halves, thirds, quarters, sixths and twelfths.

Introduction

Year 2

Tell the children that they will be using clocks to help them with their fraction work.

- Ask the children to put the hands on their clocks to divide the clocks in half.
- Demonstrate this on the OHP by displaying the acetate clock and covering half of it with half a card clock.
- Explain that you have split the clock into two parts and covered one of those two parts.
- Demonstrate that two halves make the whole.
- Ask the children to show a quarter by putting the hands on the 12 and 3 or, for the more able, other numbers.
- Demonstrate this using a quarter circle on the acetate clock, again explaining that the clock has now been split into four equal parts and that one has been covered.
- Ask the children if they can demonstrate on the OHP to the class some other places where they can make a quarter, for example 1 and 4, 6 and 9, 11 and 2.
- Demonstrate two quarters and a half, four quarters and a whole. Stress the word equivalent each time and say that you have split or divided the clock into so many equal parts and covered one or more of them.

Years 3 to 6
Again, explain that the children will be using clocks to help them with their fraction work.

- Repeat the Year 2 activities including thirds, sixths and twelfths, each time using the clock acetate and covering it with the card pieces you have prepared.

- Each time look at the equivalent fractions, i.e. halves and quarters; sixths and twelfths; thirds, sixths and twelfths.

- Keep matching how many are needed for the whole clock, for example 12 twelfths.

Activities

The children will need:

- copies of the clock from photocopiable sheet 16 on paper or card;
- scissors;
- glue;
- large paper;
- number lines (use the ones on page 33 and copy onto A3 paper).

Year 2
Give the children three copies of the clock.

- Ask them to keep one as a whole; cut another into halves and the other into quarters.

- Give them a large piece of paper and ask them to stick the whole clock, a half and a quarter, onto it and label the fractions.

- Ask them to demonstrate using some of the left-over pieces how two quarters are the same as a half.

Years 3 to 6
Give the children six copies of the clock.

- Ask them to cut one into half from the numbers 12 to 6, and stick it onto one side of a large piece of paper.

- Ask them to do the same thing to another for a quarter, another for a third, a sixth and a twelfth, labelling each one. See guidelines in Chapter 1 (page 1) for the appropriate fractions for each year group.

- Ask them to look carefully at the pieces and decide which is the smallest, the next smallest and so on, to the largest.

- Once they have decided, they need to plot them onto the first number line (copied onto A3 paper).

- With their spare pieces, ask them to cut out and stick onto paper all the equivalences to $\frac{1}{2}$, i.e. $\frac{2}{4}$, $\frac{3}{6}$, $\frac{6}{12}$, and plot these onto the second number line.

Years 3 to 6

Using the clock pieces, ask the children to cut out and glue onto large coloured paper the following fraction equivalences: $\frac{1}{3}$ and $\frac{2}{6}$, $\frac{6}{12}$ and $\frac{1}{2}$, $\frac{3}{4}$ and $\frac{9}{12}$. Ask them to make up some more. See guidelines for the appropriate fractions for your year group.

Key questions

- How many halves make a whole?
- Can you show us and explain?
- Which pieces that are the same size as each other can you make into half the clock?
- Can you demonstrate and explain?
- Can you show some equivalent fractions?
- How many minutes do these pieces represent?
- If you had pieces that were 24ths, how many minutes would each represent?

Photocopiable Sheet 16

Clock fractions

12 1 2 3 4 5 6 7 8 9 10 11

Number lines for clock activities

Plot your fractions onto this number line.

0 ____ 1

How can you show the equivalent fractions on this number line?

0 ____ 1

Chapter 6

Brainstorming fractions and percentages

This activity will encourage the children to think about how to work out percentages and fractions of numbers, including money. This can be done simply and also in an extended way, encouraging the more able children to generate their own ideas.

Preparation

Very little. All you need is a board and pen or chalk.
The children will need a large piece of paper each or to share with a partner.

Activities

Begin with a whole-class lesson on finding either fractions (Years 3 and 4) or percentages (Years 5 and 6) of amounts, then mix the two up (Years 5 and 6), ask, for example, if 100% is 100, what else can we find out? Put that information on the board as shown below and then brainstorm the children's ideas and add them to your original example. Encourage the children to discover as many facts as they can, providing prompts if necessary.

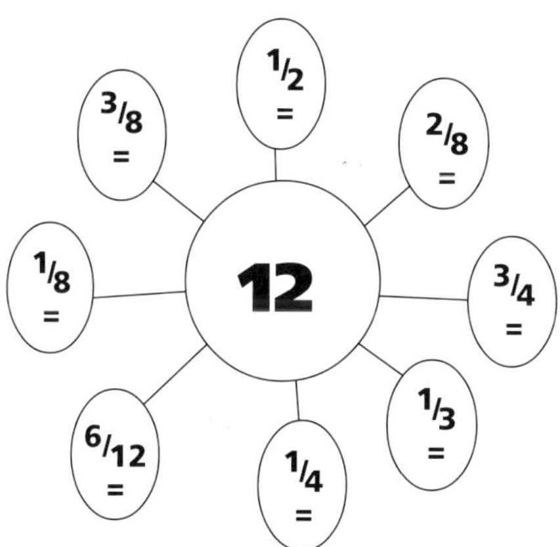

Example for Years 3 and 4

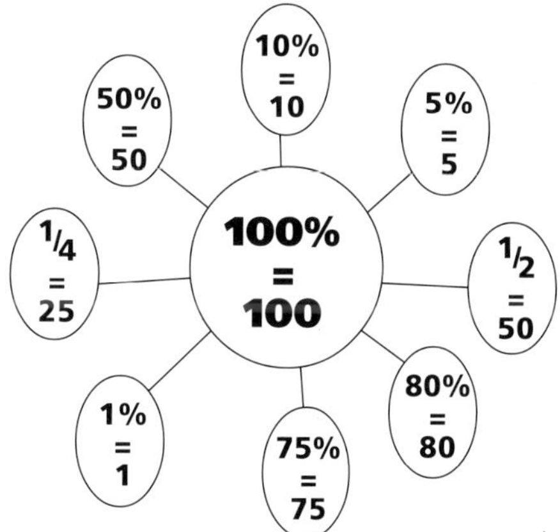

Example for Years 5 and 6, mixing percentages and fractions

> **Key questions**
>
> - If 100% equals (choose amount) what else do we know?
> - How did you work that out?

After this simple example, proceed onto a more complicated example, for example, if 100% is £140, what else can we find out?

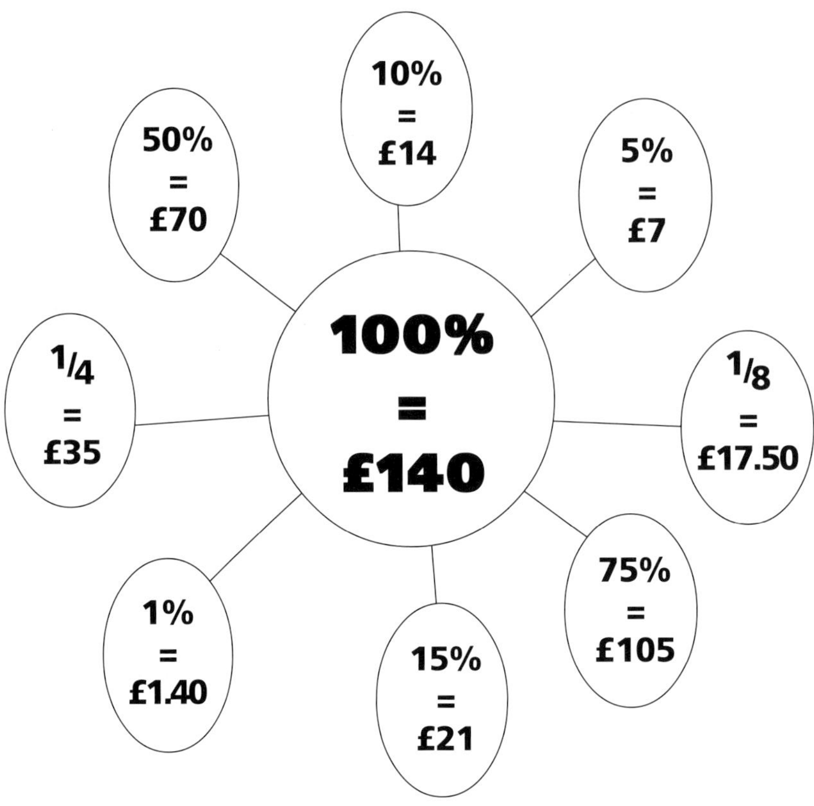

Extension

After an example such as the one above, give the children large pieces of paper and a percentage equivalent to brainstorm in pairs or individually.

The amounts that you give them should be differentiated as should the number of facts that they can work out, for example:

Year 6

Lower achieving group – 100% = 200 (finding percentages only).
Core group – 100% = £280 (fractions and percentages).
More able group – 100% = £275 (at least ten fractions and ten percentages).

Chapter 7

Make a whole

This is a game for two players suitable for Years 3 to 6.

Preparation

Each pair will need:

- a 'make a whole' strip each (use photocopiable sheets 17 and 18);
- set of fraction cards (use photocopiable sheets 19 and 20) for:
  - — Year 3 use quarters and eighths;
  - — Year 4 use halves, quarters and eighths;
  - — Year 5 use halves, thirds, sixths and twelfths;
  - — Year 6 use halves, thirds, quarters, sixths and twelfths.
- counters.

Years 3 and 4
Each player has a strip divided into eighths. They take turns to turn over the fraction cards from the pack and place counters on the sections of their strips to the number of eighths each card represents.

For example, if they pick up the ½ card, they put counters on four sections of the strip.The winner is the player who fills their strip first. If they are unable to put counters on the exact number of eighths, they miss their go.

Years 5 and 6
The same idea as above, only the strip is divided into twelfths and the fraction cards selected by you are as in the preparation section.

Key questions

- How many eighths are there in one half?
- How many eighths are there in one quarter?
- How many sixths are there in one third?
- How many twelfths are there in one quarter (etc.)?
- Can you explain how you know this?
- How did you work that out?

Photocopiable Sheet 17
Make a whole (eighths)

Pick a fraction card, place counters on the parts of your strip that are equivalent to the fraction. The winner is the first player to fill their strip. If you can't use the fraction card, you miss your go.

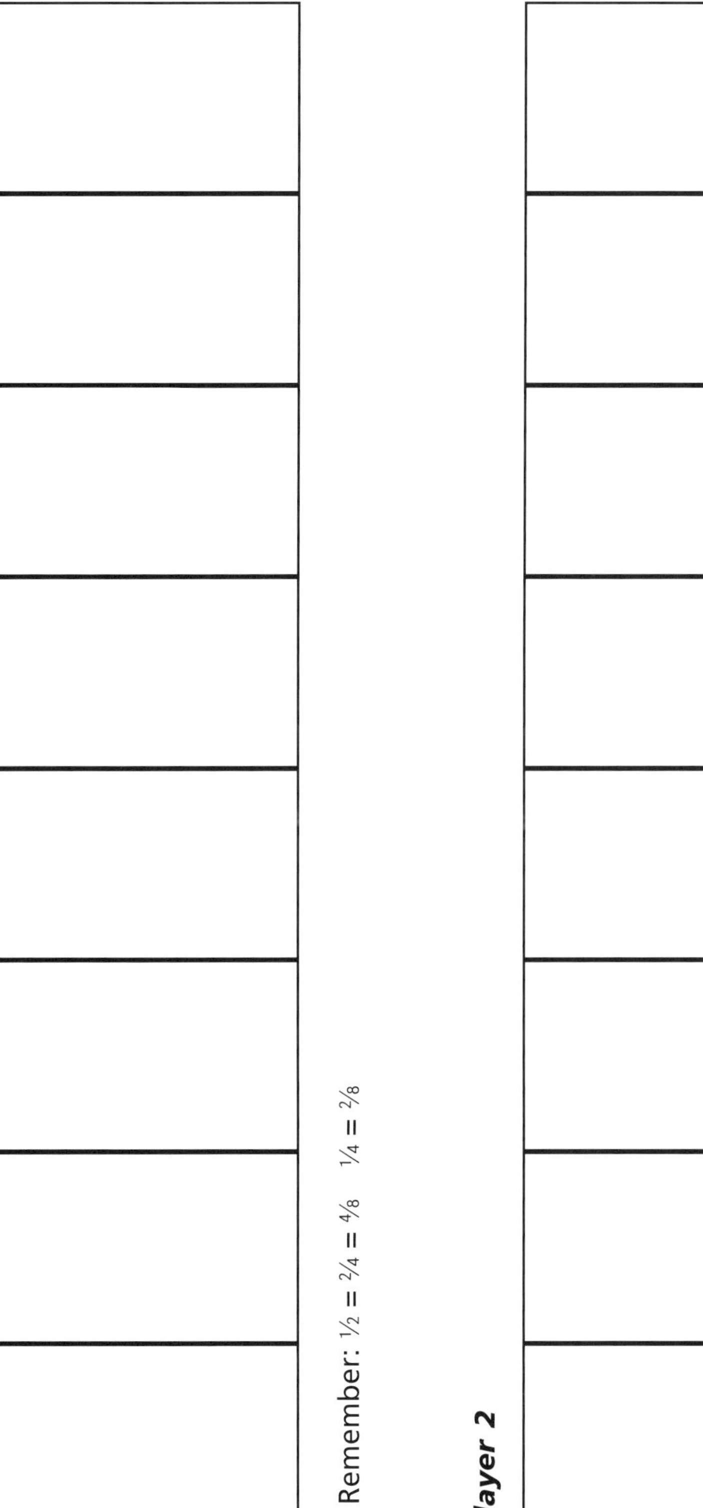

Photocopiable Sheet 18

Make a whole (twelfths)

Player 1

Remember: $\frac{1}{2} = \frac{3}{6} = \frac{6}{12}$ $\frac{2}{3} = \frac{2}{6} = \frac{8}{12}$ $\frac{1}{6} = \frac{2}{12}$

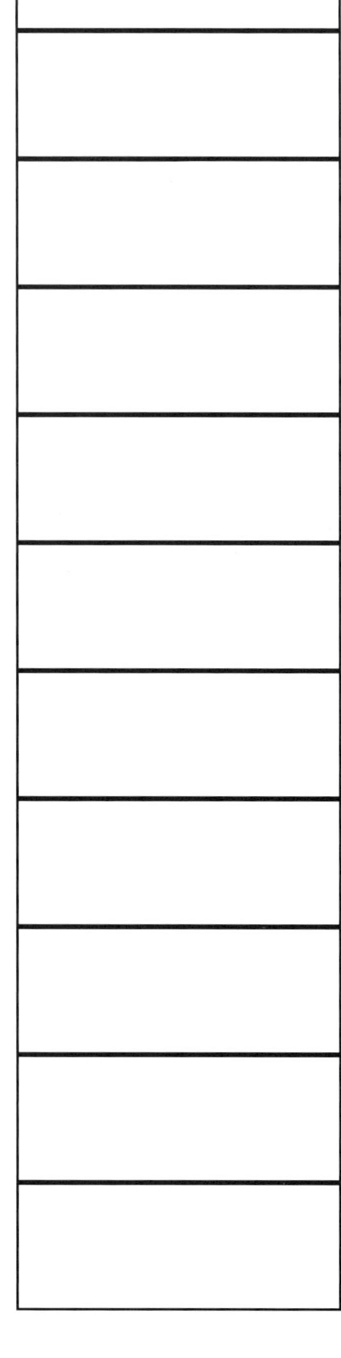

Player 2

Remember: $\frac{1}{2} = \frac{3}{6} = \frac{6}{12}$ $\frac{2}{3} = \frac{2}{6} = \frac{8}{12}$ $\frac{1}{6} = \frac{2}{12}$

Photocopiable Sheet 19

Make a whole A

Fraction cards for 'make a whole' game: Eighths

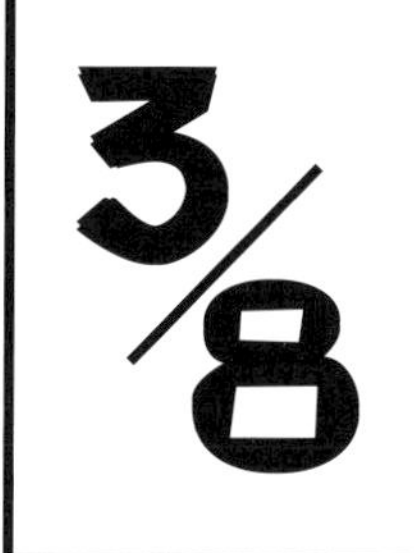

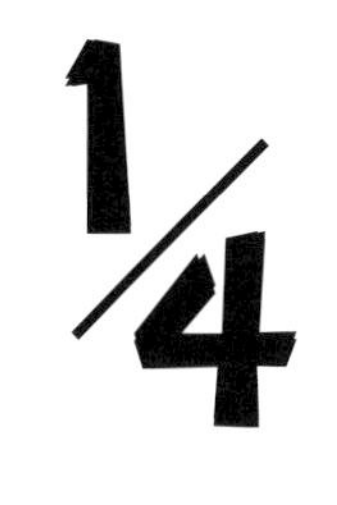

1/2

Photocopiable Sheet 20

Make a whole B

Fraction cards for 'make a whole' game: Twelfths

1/12	1/12	1/12	1/3
1/3	2/3	1/6	1/6
1/6	1/6	2/6	2/6
1/12	1/12	3/12	5/12
7/12	5/6	1/2	1/2

Chapter 8

Halving patterns

This activity encourages the children to make patterns based on halving. The results will provide plenty of material for an impressive display.

Suitable for Year 2 to Year 4 children.

Preparation

Each child will need

- three sheets of coloured A4 card:

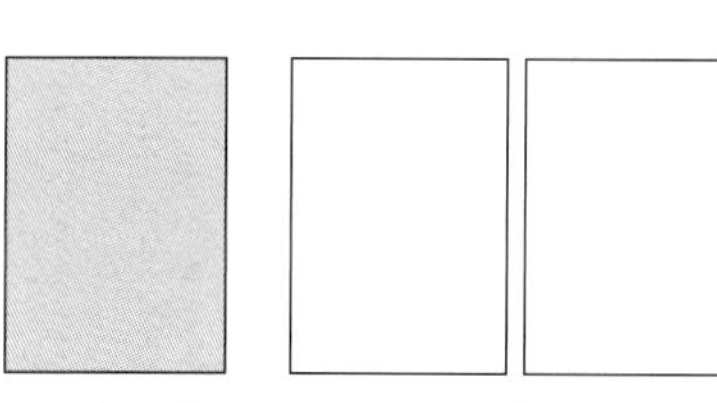

- scissors and glue.

one sheet of colour 1 | two sheets of colour 2

Activity

Use one sheet of colour 2 as the base, halve the sheet of colour 1 and stick it on to the base:

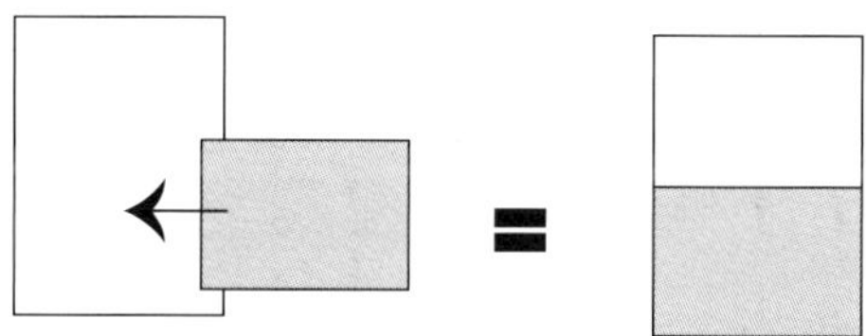

Take the other piece of colour 2 and halve it. Discard one half and halve the other, stressing that this is a quarter. Stick it onto the base:

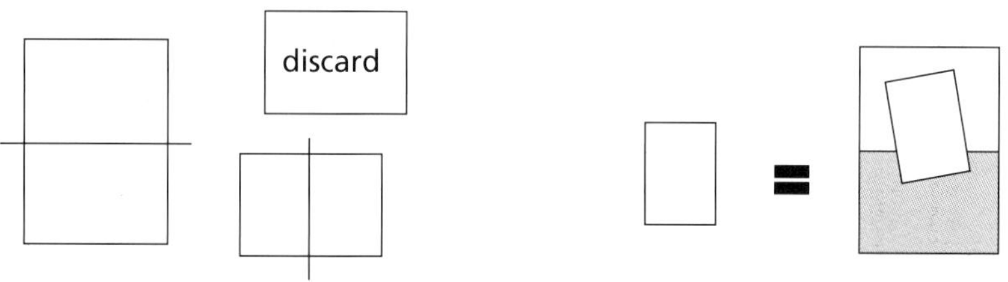

Take the remaining half of colour 1 and halve it. Discard one half and halve the other, demonstrating an eighth. Stick it onto the base:

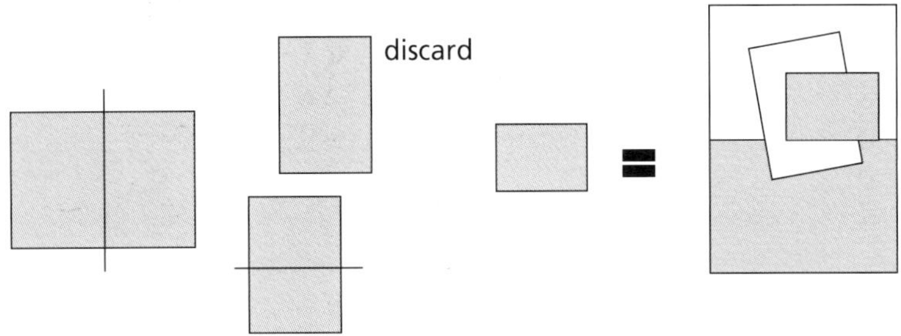

Continue doing this for sixteenths and thirty-seconds, until the children have made an abstract pattern:

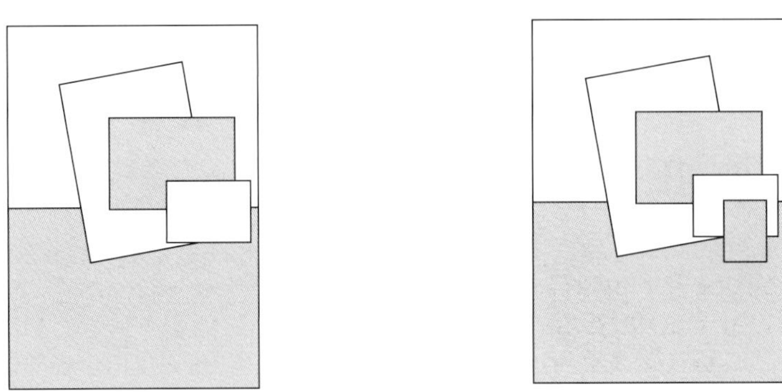

With Year 2 children take this pattern as far as quarters, or possibly eighths, asking how many halves make a whole? How many quarters make a half? With Year 3 and 4 children go as far as sixteenths or thirty seconds, asking questions like how many eighths make a half? How many sixteenths will be needed to cover a quarter of the base card?

Key questions

- How many of these pieces will make up the whole base?
- How many will be the same as half the base?
- Can you tell me how many eighths will be the same as this quarter?
- How many sixteenths are equivalent to a half?

Chapter 9

Fraction sticks

This activity extends the fraction aspects of Chapter 3 'Show me' strips, particularly looking at equivalences.

Preparation

You will need:

- selected strips from the stick sheet on acetate;
- OHP;
- thin OHP pen;
- strips cut to the same length as those on the stick sheet;
- centimetre cubes;
- centimetre squared paper for each child;
- a copy of the stick sheet for each child;
- scissors;
- coloured pencil;
- extra paper.

Introduction

Display one of the sticks from the sheet on the OHP. Put the equivalent to a centimetre cube on to it. Ask the children to estimate how many cubes will fit into the length. Try out their suggestions.

Find out if any of them can tell you what fraction one cube is of the whole strip. Demonstrate by drawing lines on the strip one cube wide and telling the children that one cube is one out of, say, eight if that is the stick you are using. Ask someone to write that fraction on the board. Do the same with the other strips. Their estimates should get more accurate as they practise.

Discuss equivalences as appropriate to the year group, for example, the six cube strip will fit twice on the 12 cube strip so that means it is $\frac{1}{2}$, $\frac{1}{2}$ is therefore equivalent to $\frac{6}{12}$.

Activity for Years 3 and 4

Each child will need:

- a copy of the stick sheet A (photocopiable sheet 21);
- a piece of centimetre squared paper;
- scissors;
- coloured pencils.

Ask the children to cut out a strip from their centimetre squared paper to match the strips on the stick sheet. Colour one square, glue them on the stick sheet in the appropriate place. Label them as a fraction, as shown below.

Activities for Years 5 and 6

Each child will need:

- copy of the stick sheet B (photocopiable sheet 22);
- a piece of centimetre squared paper;
- scissors;
- coloured pencils.

Ask them to cut out strips of the centimetre squared paper to match the sticks on the sheet. They need at least two strips of each length. They should colour each different length strip a different colour.

Next, ask them to build up the smaller strips to make the longest one and write an addition sum. For those that are able, ask them to simplify the fractions, for example:

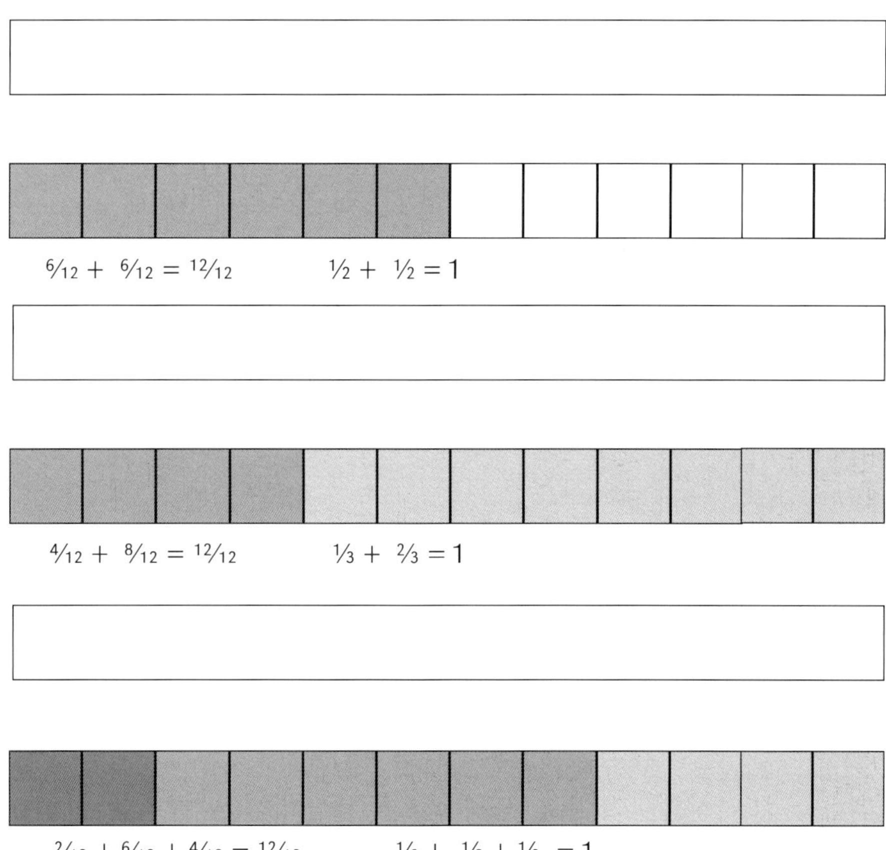

Encourage the children to investigate as many possibilities as they can.

Photocopiable Sheet 21
Stick sheet A

Cut out strips from centimetre squared paper to match the sticks. Colour one square of your strip and write down the fraction.

Stick your strip of cm^2 paper on the shaded strips.

1 square =

1 square =

1 square =

1 square =

1 square =

1 square =

1 square =

Photocopiable Sheet 22
Stick sheet B

Chapter 10

Go for five

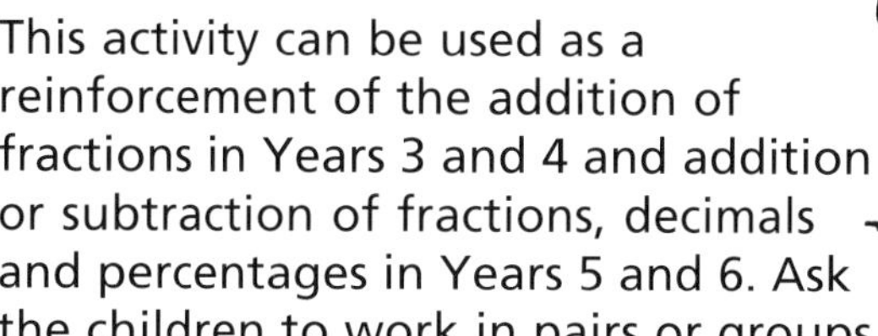

This activity can be used as a reinforcement of the addition of fractions in Years 3 and 4 and addition or subtraction of fractions, decimals and percentages in Years 5 and 6. Ask the children to work in pairs or groups of four.

Preparation

Year 3: The children will need three lots of the digit cards 1, 2, 4, and photocopiable sheet 23.

Year 4: These children will need the digit cards 1, 2, 4, 8, or 1, 2, 5 and 10, and photocopiable sheet 23.

Year 5: They will need the digit cards 1, 2, 4, 8, or 1, 5, 10, and photocopiable sheet 24.

Year 6: They will need the Year 5 equipment plus digit cards 3 and 6.

The game

Year 3

The aim of the game is to get to a score of 5. You have a maximum of ten goes. The children take it in turns to pick two digit cards and make a fraction, using the lowest card as the numerator. If they pick two cards the same they have made one whole.

They begin at 0, make their fraction, add it to their score by filling in the game sheet as shown here.

Player 1		**Player 2**	
Fraction	*Score*	*Fraction*	*Score*
$\frac{2}{4}$	$\frac{1}{2}$	$\frac{1}{2}$	$\frac{1}{2}$
$\frac{1}{1}$	$1\frac{1}{2}$	$\frac{2}{4}$	1
$\frac{1}{4}$	$1\frac{3}{4}$	$\frac{2}{2}$	2

First go: Player one picks 2 and 4, makes $\frac{2}{4}$. Player two picks 1 and 2, makes $\frac{1}{2}$.

Second go: Player one picks 1 and 1, makes whole. Player two picks 2 and 4, makes $\frac{2}{4}$.

Third go: Player one picks 1 and 4, makes $\frac{1}{4}$. Player two picks 2 and 2, makes whole.

And so on until they have had 10 goes. The player closest to 5 is the winner.

Year 4
Use digit cards 1, 2, 4, 8 or 1, 2, 5, 10 and photocopiable sheet 24.

Year 5
Use the same options for making fractions and the same rules (also getting to 5 or 500%), but this time convert them to decimals and percentages as well, as shown below:

Player 1						**Player 2**					
Fraction	*Score*	*Decimal*	*Score*	%	*Score*	*Fraction*	*Score*	*Decimal*	*Score*	%	*Score*
$\frac{2}{10}$	$\frac{1}{5}$	**0.2**	**0.2**	**20**	**20**	$\frac{2}{8}$	$\frac{1}{4}$	**0.25**	**0.25**	**25**	**25**
$\frac{1}{8}$		**0.125**	**0.325**	**12½**	**32½**	$\frac{4}{5}$		**0.20**	**0.45**	**20**	**45**

If a child cannot work out the score for the fraction coloumn, they can leave that part until it can be discussed with you. They should complete the decimal score and percentage score columns.

Year 6
Same as Year 5, but include thirds and sixths and allow subtraction to challenge the most able children. Their aim will be not to get above 5, if they do they go 'bust'.

Photocopiable Sheet 23

Go for five A

Player 1		Player 2	
Fraction	*Score*	*Fraction*	*Score*

Player 1		Player 2	
Fraction	*Score*	*Fraction*	*Score*

Photocopiable Sheet 24

Go for five B

Player 1						Player 2					
Fraction	*Score*	*Decimal*	*Score*	%	*Score*	*Fraction*	*Score*	*Decimal*	*Score*	%	*Score*

Player 1						Player 2					
Fraction	*Score*	*Decimal*	*Score*	%	*Score*	*Fraction*	*Score*	*Decimal*	*Score*	%	*Score*